Great
Salads and
Vegetables

Great
Salads and
Vegetables

Robert Carrier

Hamlyn London · New York · Sydney · Toronto

Photographs in this series taken by Christian Délu, John Miller, Jack Nisberg, Iain Reid, Pipe-Rich
Design by Martin Atcherley for The Nassington Press Ltd.
Line drawings by Ann Savage

Some material in this book has already been published in
The Robert Carrier Cookbook
Published in 1965 by
Thomas Nelson and Sons Ltd.
© Copyright Robert Carrier 1965

Published by
The Hamlyn Publishing Group Limited
London · New York · Sydney · Toronto
Astronaut House, Feltham, Middlesex, England

© Copyright Robert Carrier 1978

ISBN 0 600 32013 8

Printed in Italy

Contents

Useful Facts and Figures

Notes on metrication

When making any of the recipes in this book, only follow one set of measures as they are not interchangeable.

In this book quantities are given in metric and Imperial measures. Exact conversion from Imperial to metric measures does not usually give very convenient working quantities and so the metric measures have been rounded off into units of 25 grams. The table below shows the recommended equivalents.

Ounces	Approx gram to nearest whole figure	Recommended conversion to nearest unit of 25
1	28	25
2	57	50
3	85	75
4	113	100
5	142	150
6	170	175
7	198	200
8	227	225
9	255	250
10	283	275
11	312	300
12	340	350
13	368	375
14	396	400
15	425	425
16 (1 lb)	454	450
17	482	475
18	510	500
19	539	550
20 (1¼ lb)	567	575

Note: When converting quantities over 20 oz first add the appropriate figures in the centre column, then adjust to the nearest unit of 25. As a general guide, 1 kg (1000 g) equals 2.2 lb or about 2 lb 3 oz. This method of conversion gives good results in nearly all cases, although in certain pastry and cake recipes a more accurate conversion is necessary to produce a balanced recipe.

Liquid measures

The millilitre has been used in this book and the following table gives a few examples.

Imperial	Approx ml to nearest whole figure	Recommended ml
¼ pint	142	150 ml
½ pint	283	300 ml
¾ pint	425	450 ml
1 pint	567	600 ml
1½ pints	851	900 ml
1¾ pints	992	1000 ml (1 litre)

Can sizes

At present, cans are marked with the exact (usually to the nearest whole number) metric equivalent of the Imperial weight of the contents, so we have followed this practice when giving can sizes.

Oven temperatures

The table below gives recommended equivalents.

	°C	°F	Gas Mark
Very cool	110	225	$\frac{1}{4}$
	120	250	$\frac{1}{2}$
Cool	140	275	1
	150	300	2
Moderate	160	325	3
	180	350	4
Moderately hot	190	375	5
	200	400	6
Hot	220	425	7
	230	450	8
Very hot	240	475	9

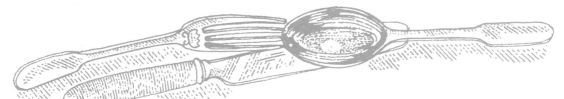

Notes for American and Australian users

In America the 8-oz measuring cup is used. In Australia metric measures are now used in conjunction with the standard 250-ml measuring cup. The Imperial pint, used in Britain and Australia, is 20 fl oz, while the American pint is 16 fl oz. It is important to remember that the Australian tablespoon differs from both the British and American tablespoons; the table below gives a comparison. The British standard tablespoon, which has been used throughout this book, holds 17.7 ml, the American 14.2 ml, and the Australian 20 ml. A teaspoon holds approximately 5 ml in all three countries.

British	American	Australian
1 teaspoon	1 teaspoon	1 teaspoon
1 tablespoon	1 tablespoon	1 tablespoon
2 tablespoons	3 tablespoons	2 tablespoons
$3\frac{1}{2}$ tablespoons	4 tablespoons	3 tablespoons
4 tablespoons	5 tablespoons	$3\frac{1}{2}$ tablespoons

An Imperial/American guide to solid and liquid measures

Solid measures

Imperial	American
1 lb butter or margarine	2 cups
1 lb flour	4 cups
1 lb granulated or castor sugar	2 cups
1 lb icing sugar	3 cups
8 oz rice	1 cup

Liquid measures

Imperial	American
$\frac{1}{4}$ pint liquid	$\frac{2}{3}$ cup liquid
$\frac{1}{2}$ pint	$1\frac{1}{4}$ cups
$\frac{3}{4}$ pint	2 cups
1 pint	$2\frac{1}{2}$ cups
$1\frac{1}{2}$ pints	$3\frac{3}{4}$ cups
2 pints	5 cups ($2\frac{1}{2}$ pints)

Introduction

Are we slated to be the last generation to savour the new, fresh tastes of spring? Is modern science, in giving us year-round bounty, robbing us of the taste sensations of the first tender asparagus, the delicate flavour and texture of fresh garden peas and tomatoes sun-ripened on the vine? Are we to forgo the crisp raw delights of tiny radishes, baby cucumbers and little new carrots?

Today, the season of everything has been stretched, so that if we were to prepare a calendar of when the majority of salads and vegetables were available in the markets, our list would undoubtedly extend from end to end of the year. Gas-stored fruit from all over the world is on sale the year round, vegetables are frozen as soon as they are picked, even game is popped into deep-freeze by amateurs, so that what were delights of a few weeks of the year now rumble on, half unnoticed, from January to December.

Of course, the convenience of this year-round bounty is enormous. Today, we could not do without our perennially present tomatoes, lettuce, celery and green peppers. These year-round stand-bys, together with our frozen and canned foods from all over the world, all help in the daily planning of our menus. But must we – in the first flush of excitement over the immense potential of accelerated freeze-drying – forget the subtle, wistful pleasures of seasonal foods?

I am afraid that when it comes to eating, I am a traditionalist; I want my tastes seasonally inspired. I like to feel the months rolling by. I want to make the most of the tender new spring vegetables: tiny new potatoes of the season's first digging, each one a fragile melting mouthful, served with mint or dill, and lemon butter; fresh garden peas, twice as sweet as the later, full-blown ones, simmered in butter with bacon, tiny white onions and shredded lettuce; carrots and mushrooms so young that a few minutes of gentle cooking in butter, or butter and cream, brings them to the peak of perfection.

To Prepare Salads

Cos lettuce, endive, chicory, young and tender spinach leaves, watercress and French *mâche* (Lamb's lettuce) all make wonderful additives to a green salad. For a little variation in texture, add sliced or chopped celery, green pepper or fennel; or flavour with finely chopped shallots and chives, especially good with diced or finely sliced avocado pear. Epicures like to eat the avocado pear *au naturel* with just a touch of simple French dressing to fill the cavity. Try scoring the meat of the avocado into cubes with a knife before adding the dressing; this allows all the flavour of your dressing to permeate the avocado rather than remaining just on top. The cut squares look attractive too. In Britain, where we often get our avocados unripe, I like to dice the delicate buttery meat of the fruit: remove it entirely from the shell, and marinate it in French dressing with a hint of finely chopped chives. Then just before serving, refill the crisp green shells with the diced cubes which have been 'tenderised' and flavoured by the French dressing marinade.

I like salads, too, as a complete meal in themselves . . . the perfect answer for summer luncheons in the country when served with hot garlic bread and followed by a mammoth tray of cheeses and a cooling sweet. **Duck and orange salad** is a delicious example – tender nuggets of duck and orange segments and celery set in a bed of lettuce with spheres of jewel-bright black olives; or **Italian cauliflower salad** with a tangy anchovy dressing. Such salads are a boon to the host or hostess, for much of the preliminary preparation of meats, vegetables or poultry can be done the day before. Of course, tired lettuce or an indiscriminate sprinkling of left-over meat and vegetables is guaranteed to take the heart out of any salad. So make your salads with the best and freshest ingredients only . . . and with a watchful eye for colour, taste and texture contrast.

Asparagus, that most delicate of spring vegetables, I like thoroughly washed or scraped (they can be gritty), then simply steamed with the smallest amount of water and served hot with melted butter or Hollandaise sauce, or *à la polonaise*. I think asparagus is important in its own right and should be served separately as a hot or cold *hors-d'oeuvre*, or as a separate vegetable course.

And who can deny that a fresh, green salad is the very essence of spring? I like mine made of baby lettuces straight from the garden with the added peppery piquancy of watercress or *roquette*, bathed in an olive oil and wine vinegar dressing, with a hint of shallot and the merest breath of garlic to accent its delicate flavour. Later in the year, a little basil or *eau-de-Cologne* mint will add its touch to the harmony of the dish.

To Prepare Vegetables

Remove coarse or damaged leaves and decayed or discoloured parts from all vegetables before cooking. When freshly gathered, they should be washed just before cooking, but when bought commercially, it is often necessary to soak them in water for a short time in order to restore some of their original freshness.

Always soak close-leaved green vegetables such as cabbage, cauliflower and Brussels sprouts in water with a little lemon juice or vinegar for about 30 minutes before cooking to remove insects.

Select vegetables that are crisp, fresh-looking and colourful. No amount of cooking and attention will revive a limp, tired vegetable. It has lost its texture, a great deal of its flavour, and most of its goodness.

Do not peel vegetables unless absolutely necessary; most of the goodness is right under the skin or in the skin itself. Wash vegetables with a stiff vegetable brush or, in the case of mushrooms, tomatoes and very new potatoes, just wipe clean with a damp cloth.

Store cleaned vegetables in plastic bags or boxes in the refrigerator to keep them crisp and fresh until ready to be used. Parsley and other herbs will keep green and fresh in this way for weeks.

To Cook Vegetables

Both French and Chinese cuisines treat vegetables with the reverence they deserve, cooking them in a little butter or oil, with just enough water, stock, wine or even steam to bring out their delicate flavours and textures.

The Chinese, particularly, are masters of the art of vegetable cookery. Serve your vegetables slightly crisp as they do, and not reduced to a pulpy, colourless mass. And follow their method of cutting vegetables across the grain into small uniform pieces, so that they will cook evenly and quickly when simmered in liquid or 'stir-fried' in vegetable oil.

Steaming

The old-fashioned method of boiling vegetables in a pot full of water and then throwing the water away has much to condemn it; so many of the valuable vitamins and trace elements are lost in the water. I far prefer to steam vegetables to obtain the utmost flavour. The younger and more delicately flavoured vegetables can be cooked in this way in 15 minutes; older vegetables and more heartily flavoured vegetables can also be steamed if they are first blanched.

'Waterless' Cooking

I like to use heavy, shallow pans with tight-fitting lids for almost waterless cooking, with just a little chicken stock or water, and a little butter or olive oil to add lustre and savour. When served hot with fresh butter, freshly ground black pepper and salt, or with a lemon- or mustard-flavoured sauce, you have a dish fit for the gods.

Braising

Another very good way of cooking vegetables to preserve maximum flavour is to braise them in a shallow ovenproof casserole.

To Serve Vegetables

I have never been interested in the vegetable primarily as an accompaniment to meat or fish. Except in rare instances, potatoes or rice or noodles can do that with great ease. So take a page from the notebooks of the best French chefs, and serve vegetables as a separate course after the main course. This will allow guests to savour the flavour of meat, game or fish more fully, and permit you to add another texture and flavour surprise in your separate vegetable course.

One of the best vegetable salads in the world is chilled *haricots verts à la vinaigrette*: beans cooked in very little water with a little butter or olive oil until just tender, not mushy and overcooked, then drained and dressed with a vinaigrette dressing to which you have added finely chopped garlic and parsley. Try this, too, with broccoli or small Brussels sprouts. Delicious.

For interesting vegetable accompaniments to meat, try leeks or endive braised in oil and butter with a clove or two of garlic and a sprig of thyme; tomatoes or mushroom caps stuffed with a Provençal mixture of fresh breadcrumbs, finely chopped garlic and parsley; sliced mushrooms simmered for a moment only in butter and lemon juice with a hint of rosemary or thyme; or a noble **gratin dauphinois**, thinly sliced new potatoes cooked in cream with freshly grated Parmesan and Gruyère cheese.

Always serve vegetables as soon as possible after cooking; many lose flavour and texture if kept warm over any period of time.

Keep a vegetable juice jar for any liquid left over after cooking your vegetables. Strain the liquid into a special jar kept covered in the refrigerator for this purpose. Vegetable juices preserved in this way make wonderful flavour additives for soups, sauces and stews.

Salads

Tossed Green Salad
Illustrated on page 28

1-2 lettuces

FRENCH DRESSING
**1 tablespoon lemon juice
1-2 tablespoons wine vinegar
$\frac{1}{4}$ level teaspoon dry mustard
coarse salt and freshly ground black pepper
6-8 tablespoons olive oil**

1. Wash lettuce leaves well in a large quantity of water. They should be left whole, never cut. Drain well and dry thoroughly in a cloth or a salad basket so that there is no water on them to dilute the dressing.

2. To make French Dressing: mix together lemon juice, wine vinegar and dry mustard, and season to taste with coarse salt and freshly ground black pepper. Add olive oil, and beat with a fork until the mixture emulsifies.

3. To serve: pour French dressing into salad bowl, arrange prepared lettuce leaves on top. Then at the table, give a final toss to the ingredients to ensure that every leaf is glistening with dressing. Check seasoning and serve.

Green Salad Variations

1. Add other salad greens in season – Cos lettuce, endive, chicory, batavia, young spinach leaves, watercress and French *mâche* (Lamb's lettuce).

2. Add finely chopped garlic or shallots, or a combination of the two, to salad dressing.

3. Add fresh green herbs – finely chopped chervil, basil, tarragon, chives or *eau-de-Cologne* mint – to the dressing.

4. For crunch appeal, add diced celery, green pepper or fennel.

Tossed Green Salad with Avocado and Bacon
Tossed Green Salad with 'Turned' Potatoes
Tossed Green Salad with Poached Carrot and Turnip
    Sticks

12

Tossed Green Salad with Avocado and Bacon

1–2 lettuces
1 bunch watercress
1 clove garlic
4 level tablespoons chopped chives or green
    onions
olive oil
wine vinegar
salt and freshly ground black pepper
1 avocado pear, peeled and sliced
lemon juice
2 rashers cooked bacon, chopped

1. Wash and prepare lettuce and watercress. Shake dry in a salad basket, or dry each leaf carefully in a clean tea towel. Wrap in tea towel and allow to crisp in refrigerator until ready to use.

2. Rub wooden salad bowl with cut clove of garlic. Arrange lettuce and watercress in bowl. Chop garlic and chives finely; sprinkle over the salad and dress with an olive oil and wine vinegar dressing (3 to 4 parts oil to 1 part vinegar), and season to taste with salt and freshly ground black pepper.

3. Garnish with wedges of avocado, which you have marinated in lemon juice to prevent it from going brown, and chopped bacon. Just before serving, toss salad until each leaf is glistening.

Tossed Green Salad with 'Turned' Potatoes

1–2 lettuces
1 bunch watercress
1–2 cloves garlic
4 level tablespoons chopped chives or green
    onions
olive oil
wine vinegar
salt and freshly ground black pepper
450 g/1 lb potatoes
French Dressing (see Tossed Green Salad,
    page 11)

1. Wash and prepare lettuce and watercress.

Shake dry in a salad basket, or dry carefully in a clean tea towel. Wrap in tea towel and allow to crisp in refrigerator until ready to use.

2. Rub wooden salad bowl with cut clove of garlic. Arrange lettuce and watercress in bowl. Chop garlic and chives finely; sprinkle over the salad and dress with an olive oil and wine vinegar dressing (3 to 4 parts oil to 1 part vinegar), and season to taste with salt and freshly ground black pepper.

3. **To prepare 'turned' potatoes:** peel potatoes and cut into small 'olive' shapes with a cutter or a sharp knife. Boil 'turned' potatoes in salted boiling water until just tender. Drain and cool.

4. Toss potatoes in a well-flavoured French dressing. Add to salad and toss well.

Tossed Green Salad with Poached Carrot and Turnip Sticks

1–2 lettuces
1 bunch watercress
1–2 cloves garlic
4 level tablespoons chopped chives or
    green onions
olive oil
wine vinegar
salt and freshly ground black pepper
225 g/8 oz carrots
100 g/4 oz turnips
French Dressing (see Tossed Green Salad,
    page 11)

Prepare the green salad as in Steps 1. and 2. of Tossed Green Salad with 'Turned' Potatoes (above).

3. Peel carrots and turnips and cut into 5-mm/$\frac{1}{4}$-inch slices, lengthwise. Cut each slice into 'sticks' 5 mm/$\frac{1}{4}$ inch thick.

4. Poach carrot and turnip sticks in boiling salted water until just tender. Drain and cool.

5. Toss in a mustard-flavoured French dressing. Add to salad and toss well.

13

Tossed Green Salad with Soured Cream Dressing

1–2 lettuces
choice of salad greens:
  endive, young spinach, watercress,
  chicory, dandelion, mâche (Lamb's
  lettuce), etc.
1 clove garlic, finely chopped
1 level teaspoon each finely chopped fresh
  basil, marjoram, chervil and chives

SOURED CREAM DRESSING
150 ml/¼ pint soured cream
2 tablespoons tarragon vinegar
¼ level teaspoon dry mustard
¼ level teaspoon sugar
salt and freshly ground black pepper

1. Wash and prepare lettuce and salad greens of your choice. Shake dry in a salad basket, or dry each leaf carefully in a clean tea towel. Wrap in tea towel and allow to crisp in refrigerator until ready to use.

2. To make Soured Cream Dressing: whip soured cream until smooth with tarragon vinegar, dry mustard, sugar and salt and freshly ground black pepper.

3. Arrange lettuce and salad greens in bowl. Sprinkle finely chopped garlic and herbs over salad and dress with soured cream dressing.

Tossed Green Salad with Mushrooms and Chives

2 lettuces
6 mushrooms
juice of ½ lemon
olive oil
wine vinegar
coarse salt and freshly ground black pepper
1 clove garlic, finely chopped
2–3 level tablespoons chopped chives

1. Wash and prepare lettuce. Shake dry in a salad basket, or dry each leaf carefully in a clean tea towel. Wrap in tea towel and allow to crisp

in the refrigerator until ready to use.

2. Arrange lettuce leaves in bowl.

3. Wash mushrooms; trim stems and slice thinly. Toss in equal quantities of lemon juice and olive oil, to preserve colour.

4. Make a well-flavoured French dressing (using 3 to 4 parts olive oil to 1 part wine vinegar) and season to taste with coarse salt and freshly ground black pepper. Stir in chopped garlic and chives and pour over salad.

5. Add sliced mushrooms and toss salad until each leaf is glistening.

Salade Niçoise I
Illustrated on page 28

4 tomatoes, seeded and quartered
½ Spanish onion, sliced
1 sweet green pepper, sliced
8 radishes
2 hearts of lettuce, cut into segments
4 sticks celery, sliced
1 (198-g/7-oz) can tuna fish, drained
8 anchovy fillets
2–3 hard-boiled eggs, quartered
black olives

SALAD DRESSING
2 tablespoons wine vinegar or lemon juice
6 tablespoons pure olive oil
salt and freshly ground black pepper
12 leaves fresh basil, coarsely chopped

1. Combine prepared vegetables in a salad bowl, placing neatly on top the tuna fish, anchovy fillets and quartered eggs. Garnish with black olives.

2. Mix salad dressing of wine vinegar, olive oil, seasoning and coarsely chopped fresh basil, and sprinkle over the salad.

Salade Niçoise II

14

1 lettuce
225 g/8 oz crisply-cooked green beans
150 ml/¼ pint well-flavoured French
    Dressing (see Tossed Green Salad, page
    11)
3 medium-sized potatoes, cooked, peeled
    and sliced
1 (198-g/7-oz) can tuna fish, drained
3 hard-boiled eggs, shelled and quartered
3 large tomatoes, cut into quarters
6 black olives
6 anchovy fillets, drained and cut into small
    pieces
juice of 1 lemon
salt and freshly ground black pepper
150 ml/¼ pint Mayonnaise (see page 91)

1. Wash lettuce and shake dry.

2. Arrange lettuce leaves in the centre of a large round platter or shallow salad bowl.

3. Cut cooked green beans into 2.5-cm/1-inch segments and toss in well-flavoured French dressing. Drain. Then toss sliced cooked potatoes in French dressing.

4. Arrange cooked green beans and sliced potatoes in alternate mounds around lettuce-lined dish. Break tuna fish into bite-sized pieces and pile in middle of salad. Garnish salad with egg and tomato slices. Sprinkle with black olives and anchovy fillets.

5. Mix lemon juice with mayonnaise and season generously with salt and freshly ground black pepper. Serve dressing separately.

Lettuce Hearts 'La Napoule'

2 small tight lettuces

'LA NAPOULE' DRESSING
6-8 tablespoons olive oil
2-3 tablespoons wine vinegar
½ level teaspoon paprika
150 ml/¼ pint double cream
salt and freshly ground black pepper

GARNISH
2 hard-boiled eggs
2 level tablespoons finely chopped parsley

1. Wash and trim lettuce and cut hearts into quarters. Drain well, wrap in a clean tea towel and pat dry. Gather up the edges and corners of the

towel, and shake out any remaining moisture. Chill in the refrigerator until crisp.

2. To make 'La Napoule' Dressing: combine olive oil, wine vinegar, paprika and double cream, season to taste with salt and freshly ground black pepper, and whisk until creamy and thick.

3. To prepare garnish: separate yolks from whites of hard-boiled eggs and rub yolks and whites separately through a wire sieve. Chop parsley.

4. To serve: place 2 quarters of lettuce on each salad plate. Mask each quarter of lettuce with dressing and garnish a third of each portion with sieved egg white, a third with sieved egg yolks, and the remaining third with finely chopped parsley.

Chilled Watercress Salad

2 bunches watercress
2 oranges

CURRY DRESSING
6–8 tablespoons olive oil
2 tablespoons wine vinegar
1 tablespoon lemon juice
1 level tablespoon curry powder
salt and freshly ground black pepper
1 level teaspoon finely chopped shallots

1. Prepare watercress; chill in a damp tea towel. Peel oranges, cut into thin segments, and chill.

2. To make Curry Dressing: combine olive oil, wine vinegar, lemon juice and curry powder. Season to taste with salt and freshly ground black pepper. Chill.

3. Just before serving, place watercress in a salad bowl, arrange orange segments on top, add finely chopped shallots to Curry Dressing and pour over salad. Toss at table so that each leaf is glistening.

Watercress and Tomato Salad

15

2 bunches watercress
4–6 ripe tomatoes, peeled, seeded and diced
½ cucumber, peeled, seeded and diced
4 sticks celery, sliced
salt and freshly ground black pepper
French Dressing (see Tossed Green Salad, page 11)
1 clove garlic, finely chopped (optional)

1. Wash and pick over the watercress, drain well and wrap in a tea towel. Chill.

2. Make French dressing and flavour with a finely chopped clove of garlic if desired.

3. When ready to serve, turn out into a large salad bowl. Arrange prepared tomatoes, cucumber and celery in centre, season to taste with salt and freshly ground black pepper, and toss with French dressing.

Raw Spinach Salad

450 g/1 lb raw spinach leaves
6–8 tablespoons olive oil
2–3 tablespoons wine vinegar
1 clove garlic, finely chopped
1–2 level tablespoons finely chopped parsley
salt and freshly ground black pepper
dry mustard
2 hard-boiled eggs, cut in quarters
1 ripe avocado pear, peeled and sliced
1 small onion, thinly sliced

1. Wash spinach several times in cold water (spinach should be young and tender). Cut off stems, drain and chill until ready to use.

2. Make a dressing with olive oil, wine vinegar and finely chopped garlic and parsley, and add salt, freshly ground black pepper and dry mustard, to taste.

3. Arrange spinach leaves in a salad bowl. Pour dressing over them; toss salad well and garnish with quartered hard-boiled eggs, sliced avocado and onion rings.

Wilted Lettuce and Bacon Salad *Serves 4 to 6*
Caesar's Salad with Mushrooms *Serves 4 to 6*
Danish Cucumber Salad *Serves 6*
Cucumber and Nasturtium Leaf Salad *Serves 4 to 6*

16

Wilted Lettuce and Bacon Salad

1–2 lettuces
4 rashers bacon
2 tablespoons olive oil
2 tablespoons wine vinegar
salt and freshly ground black pepper
1 level teaspoon sugar
2 level tablespoons chopped green onions

1. Prepare lettuce.

2. Cook the bacon in olive oil in a frying pan until crisp and brown. Remove bacon and chop finely.

3. Stir wine vinegar into the hot fat. Add salt, freshly ground black pepper and sugar. Mix well.

4. Place lettuce leaves in salad bowl. Pour over warm bacon fat and vinegar dressing. Toss well. Sprinkle with crumbled bacon and chopped green onions.

Caesar's Salad with Mushrooms
Illustrated on page 28

1 Cos lettuce
6–8 tablespoons olive oil
2 tablespoons wine vinegar
6 level tablespoons finely grated Parmesan
   cheese
1–2 fat cloves garlic, mashed
salt and freshly ground black pepper
lemon juice
6 button mushrooms, sliced
2 slices bread, diced
2 level tablespoons butter
2 raw egg yolks
6 anchovy fillets

1. Prepare Cos lettuce; wash and drain.

2. Combine olive oil, wine vinegar, grated cheese and garlic in a large salad bowl and season to taste with salt, freshly ground black pepper and lemon juice. Add sliced mushrooms and toss.

3. Sauté diced bread in butter with a little garlic.

4. Add torn lettuce to salad bowl, and toss lightly. Then add egg yolks and toss salad until every leaf glistens. Top off with garlic-flavoured fried bread *croûtons* and anchovy fillets.

Danish Cucumber Salad

2 cucumbers
1 level tablespoon salt
water and wine vinegar
2 level tablespoons sugar
white pepper
2 level tablespoons finely chopped parsley

1. Peel and slice cucumbers very finely. Sprinkle with salt and place under a weight in a glass bowl for at least 1 hour. Wash well. Drain and dry thoroughly with a clean tea towel.

2. Combine water and wine vinegar, to taste; add sugar and white pepper and pour over cucumber slices. Leave salad in the refrigerator for 1 hour.

3. Just before serving, sprinkle with finely chopped parsley. Serve with grilled or fried meat, fish or chicken.

Cucumber and Nasturtium Leaf Salad

1 cucumber
36 small nasturtium leaves
1 level teaspoon Dijon mustard
2 tablespoons wine vinegar
6 tablespoons olive oil
salt and freshly ground black pepper
2 level tablespoons finely chopped fresh
   tarragon
6 nasturtium flowers (optional)

1. Peel and slice cucumber thinly. Wash nasturtium leaves, remove stems and drain.

2. Combine mustard and vinegar in a bowl and stir until well blended. Add olive oil, salt and freshly ground black pepper to taste, and blend well. Stir in tarragon.

3. When ready to serve, combine cucumber and nasturtium leaves in a salad bowl. Add dressing and toss well. Garnish with nasturtium flowers, if desired.

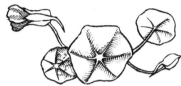

Raw Vegetable Salad with Green Dressing

12 baby carrots
12 baby turnips
12 baby beets
6 tablespoons well-flavoured French Dressing (see Tossed Green Salad, page 11)
lettuce leaves (1 lettuce)
12 radishes

GREEN DRESSING
150 ml/¼ pint soured cream
4 level tablespoons sliced green onions
lemon juice
salt and freshly ground black pepper
green food colouring

1. Wash fresh new vegetables from your garden: carrots, turnips and beets. Do not peel. Put them through the finest blade of your *mouli-légumes* to make long thin threads. Do beets last as they tend to stain other vegetables. Toss each vegetable separately in 2 tablespoons French dressing.

2. Wash and dry lettuce leaves. Arrange them around a large, shallow bowl. Pile each vegetable separately in centre of bowl, according to colour. Place washed and sliced radishes in centre. Serve with Green Dressing.

3. To make Green Dressing: combine soured cream with sliced green onions and a little lemon juice, salt and freshly ground black pepper, to taste. Whisk until smooth. Add a few drops green food colouring.

French Celery Appetiser Salad

17

2 heads celery
1 chicken stock cube
1 level tablespoon salt

VINAIGRETTE SAUCE
coarse salt and freshly ground black pepper
2 tablespoons wine vinegar
6-8 tablespoons olive oil
½ level teaspoon paprika
cayenne
150 ml/¼ pint double cream

GARNISH
4 hard-boiled eggs
4 level tablespoons finely chopped parsley

1. Trim heads of celery, cutting off top third and outside sticks. Cut each head in half and put in a saucepan with trimmings, chicken stock cube and salt. Cover with cold water and bring slowly to the boil. Simmer for 10 minutes. Remove from heat and leave in stock for 5 minutes. Drain and cool.

2. To make Vinaigrette Sauce: add coarse salt and freshly ground black pepper to wine vinegar, to taste. Stir the mixture well. Add olive oil and beat with a fork until the mixture thickens.

3. Arrange blanched celery halves in a flat dish. Spoon over half the vinaigrette sauce and allow celery to marinate in this mixture for at least 1 hour.

4. Combine remaining vinaigrette sauce with paprika, a pinch of cayenne and double cream. Mix well.

5. To prepare the garnish: separate yolks from whites of eggs, and rub each separately through a wire sieve.

6. To serve: place celery halves on a serving dish and cover with Vinaigrette Sauce. Garnish one-third of each celery half with sieved egg white, one-third with sieved egg yolk, and remaining third with finely chopped parsley. Serve immediately.

18

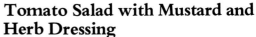

Tomato Salad with Mustard and Herb Dressing

4-6 large tomatoes
lemon juice
salt and freshly ground black pepper
1 bunch watercress

MUSTARD AND HERB DRESSING
2 tablespoons wine vinegar
1 level teaspoon dry mustard
1 small clove garlic, finely chopped
2 level tablespoons chopped chives
2 level tablespoons chopped parsley
2 level tablespoons chopped tarragon
6-8 tablespoons olive oil
salt and freshly ground black pepper

Tomato Salad with Basil

4 large tomatoes
salt and freshly ground black pepper
8 level tablespoons finely chopped echalote
   rose, or finely chopped onion or spring
   onions
4 level tablespoons finely chopped basil
   leaves
4 level tablespoons finely chopped tarragon
   leaves
4 level tablespoons finely chopped parsley
olive oil
wine vinegar
Dijon mustard

1. Wash tomatoes and cut in half horizontally.
Arrange tomato halves, cut side up, on a serving
dish and season generously with salt and freshly
ground black pepper.

2. Sprinkle each tomato half with finely chopped
echalote rose (or finely chopped onion or spring
onions). Mix fresh herbs together and sprinkle
each tomato half with a thick green layer of
chopped herbs.

3. Make a well-flavoured French dressing (3 parts
olive oil to 1 part wine vinegar, Dijon mustard
and salt and freshly ground black pepper, to taste).
Dribble 2 to 3 tablespoons dressing over each
tomato half.

1. Wash tomatoes and cut into quarters. Place
them in a bowl with lemon juice, salt and freshly
ground black pepper, to taste. Wash and trim
watercress.

2. To make Mustard and Herb Dressing:
combine wine vinegar and mustard in a small
bowl. Add finely chopped garlic and fresh herbs.
Beat in olive oil and season to taste with salt and
freshly ground black pepper. At the last moment,
whisk an ice cube in dressing for a second or two
to thicken emulsion. Remove cube.

3. To assemble salad: drain tomatoes and
arrange in a shallow salad bowl. Garnish with
watercress and pour over Mustard and Herb
Dressing.

Celeriac Salad with Mustard Dressing

2 celery roots (celeriac)
salt

MUSTARD DRESSING
6-8 level tablespoons double cream
2 tablespoons olive oil
2-3 tablespoons lemon juice
1 level tablespoon finely chopped onion
dry mustard
salt and freshly ground black pepper

1. Cook celeriac in boiling salted water until tender. Cool. Peel and cut into thin strips.

2. **To make Mustard Dressing:** combine cream, olive oil, lemon juice and finely chopped onion, and dry mustard, salt and freshly ground black pepper, to taste. Blend well.

3. Marinate celeriac in Mustard Dressing overnight in the refrigerator.

Fresh Asparagus Salad

24 sticks fresh asparagus, cooked
150 ml/¼ pint well-flavoured French
    Dressing (see Tossed Green Salad, page
    11)
salt and freshly ground black pepper
1 lettuce
1 bunch watercress, or 6 Cos or escarole
    leaves
6-12 thin strips canned pimento
3 hard-boiled eggs, sliced in half

1. Cut cooked asparagus into 5-cm/2-inch lengths. Toss in half the French dressing; season generously with salt and freshly ground black pepper and chill until ready to serve.

2. **When ready to serve:** arrange lettuce leaves around the edges of a large flat serving dish or shallow salad bowl. Garnish with sprigs of watercress, or Cos or *escarole* leaves. Place marinated asparagus segments in the centre of the dish and garnish dish with thin strips of pimento and hard-boiled egg halves. Sprinkle salad with remaining French dressing and serve immediately.

Italian Cauliflower Salad

1 cauliflower
salt

ITALIAN DRESSING
4 anchovy fillets, finely chopped
150 ml/¼ pint olive oil
juice of 1 lemon
salt and freshly ground black pepper

1. Remove green leaves from cauliflower, trim stem and cut out any bruised spots. Break or cut into flowerets and poach in lightly salted water for about 5 minutes. Drain and place in a bowl of cold salted water until ready to use. Drain well.

2. **To make Italian Dressing:** mix finely chopped anchovy fillets with olive oil and lemon juice and season to taste with salt and freshly ground black pepper.

3. When ready to serve, mix flowerets thoroughly with Italian Dressing.

Courgette Salad

12 courgettes
salt
French Dressing (see Tossed Green Salad,
    page 11)
finely chopped parsley, chervil or tarragon

1. Cut unpeeled courgettes into thick slices or quarters and blanch in boiling salted water for 6 to 8 minutes. Drain well and chill.

2. Just before serving, place courgettes in a salad bowl, add a well-flavoured French dressing and sprinkle lightly with finely chopped parsley, chervil or tarragon.

19

St Tropez Salad 'Aux Frottes d'Ail' *Serves 4 to 6*
Austrian Potato Salad *Serves 4*
Potato Salad with Bacon and Frankfurters
Serves 4 to 6

20

St. Tropez Salad 'Aux Frottes d'Ail'

8 thin slices French bread
2-4 cloves garlic
coarse salt
olive oil
8 anchovy fillets
wine vinegar
Dijon mustard
salt and freshly ground black pepper
1 curly endive
4 hard-boiled eggs, cut in halves
black olives

1. Slice French bread into thin rounds. Dry in oven and then rub each with garlic. Sprinkle with coarse salt and olive oil, using about 4 tablespoons olive oil. Place 1 anchovy fillet on each round.

2. Make a mustard-flavoured French dressing (6 to 8 tablespoons olive oil, 2 to 3 tablespoons wine vinegar, $\frac{1}{2}$ to 1 level teaspoon Dijon mustard, finely chopped garlic and salt and freshly ground black pepper, to taste). Add prepared curly endive and toss until each leaf glistens with dressing.

3. Garnish salad with garlic rubbed bread and halved hard-boiled eggs. Sprinkle with black olives.

Austrian Potato Salad

1-1$\frac{1}{2}$ kg/2-3 lb new potatoes
salt
4-6 slices ham, diced
chopped gherkins
150 ml/$\frac{1}{4}$ pint double cream
4 level tablespoons Mayonnaise (see
  page 91)

1. Scrub new potatoes. Cook in boiling salted water until just tender – 15 to 20 minutes. Drain, peel and slice. Place potatoes in a bowl, add diced ham and chopped gherkins.

2. Combine double cream and mayonnaise. Pour over potatoes and toss gently.

Potato Salad with Bacon and Frankfurters

1-1$\frac{1}{2}$ kg/2-3 lb new potatoes
salt
1 level tablespoon sugar
2 tablespoons wine vinegar
4-6 rashers bacon
olive oil
4 cooked frankfurters, thinly sliced
lemon juice
2-4 level tablespoons finely chopped onion
2-4 level tablespoons finely chopped parsley
salt and cayenne

1. Scrub new potatoes. Cook in boiling salted water until just tender – 15 to 20 minutes. Drain, peel and slice.

2. Place potatoes in a bowl and sprinkle with sugar and wine vinegar. Toss gently.

3. Sauté bacon in a little oil until crisp. Drain well, pouring bacon fat over potatoes. Crumble or chop bacon finely and add to potatoes. Add sliced frankfurters and toss gently.

4. Combine 6 tablespoons olive oil with lemon juice, to taste, and finely chopped onion and parsley. Season to taste with salt and cayenne. Pour over salad. Toss well. Correct seasoning, adding more olive oil, lemon juice, salt or cayenne, if desired.

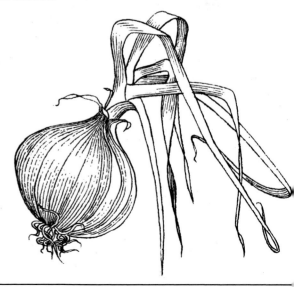

Cooked Vegetable Salad I

6 medium-sized carrots, cooked
4 new potatoes, cooked
225 g/8 oz green beans, cooked
1 (113-g/4-oz) packet frozen peas, cooked
salt and freshly ground black pepper
2 level tablespoons finely chopped onion
2 level tablespoons finely chopped parsley
150 ml/¼ pint French Dressing (see Tossed
   Green Salad, page 11)
lettuce leaves (1 lettuce)
1 bunch watercress, or 6 Cos leaves
   (optional)
2 tomatoes, cut into wedges

1. Slice carrots. Peel and slice new potatoes. Cut cooked green beans into 2½-cm/1-inch segments. Combine these vegetables in a bowl with peas.

2. Season generously with salt and freshly ground black pepper. Add finely chopped onion and parsley and half the French dressing and toss well. Refrigerate until ready to serve.

3. When ready to serve: arrange lettuce leaves around the edges of a large flat serving dish or shallow salad bowl. Garnish with sprigs of watercress or dark Cos leaves. Mound vegetable salad in the centre of leaves and garnish with tomato wedges. Sprinkle salad with remaining French dressing and serve immediately.

Cooked Vegetable Salad II

21

6 large carrots
3 young turnips
3 large new potatoes
salt
225 g/8 oz string beans
½ cauliflower
6 tablespoons cooked peas
2 level tablespoons finely chopped parsley
150 ml/¼ pint French Dressing (see Tossed
   Green Salad, page 11)

1. Scoop balls from raw carrots, turnips and potatoes with a potato scoop (or cut into cubes), and cook them in boiling salted water until tender but still firm – about 5 or 6 minutes. Drain and cool.

2. Cut string beans into 2.5-cm/1-inch lengths and cook as above until tender but still firm. Drain and cool.

3. Break cauliflower into flowerets and cook as above until tender but still firm. Drain and cool.

4. Combine cooked vegetables and toss with French dressing. Sprinkle with finely chopped parsley.

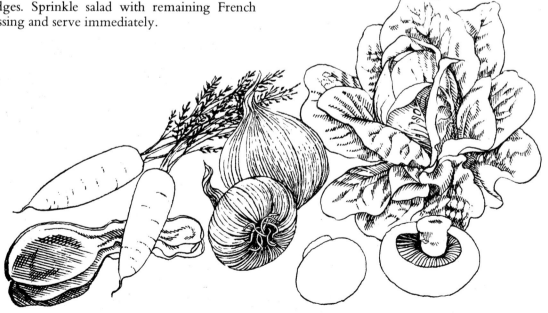

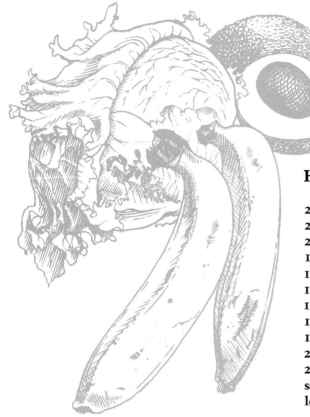

Julienne Salad

1-2 lettuces
225 g/8 oz smoked ox tongue
225 g/8 oz cooked ham
225 g/8 oz Swiss cheese
3 hard-boiled eggs, cut in quarters
6 tomatoes, cut in wedges
1 bunch watercress
French Dressing (see Tossed Green Salad,
 page 11)

1. Wash and dry lettuces carefully, leaf by leaf. Chop coarsely and arrange in the bottom of a large salad bowl.

2. Cut tongue, ham and cheese into thin strips and arrange according to colour on bed of lettuce with hard-boiled eggs and raw tomatoes.

3. Place a cluster of prepared watercress in centre of salad and serve with a well-flavoured French dressing.

Ham and Chicken Salad

225 g/8 oz cooked ham, diced
225 g/8 oz cooked chicken, diced
2 bananas, sliced
1 orange, separated into segments
1 avocado pear, peeled and sliced
150 ml/¼ pint double cream
150 ml/¼ pint Mayonnaise (see page 91)
1-2 level tablespoons ketchup
1 teaspoon Worcestershire sauce
2 tablespoons lemon juice
2 tablespoons brandy
salt and freshly ground black pepper
lettuce leaves

1. Combine diced cooked ham and chicken with sliced bananas, orange and avocado segments in a mixing bowl.

2. Whip the cream and blend in mayonnaise. Add ketchup, Worcestershire sauce, lemon juice and brandy, and pour over meat and fruit mixture. Season to taste with salt and freshly ground black pepper, and mix carefully. Serve on lettuce leaves.

Ham and Apple Salad

1 slice ham, 1 cm/½ inch thick
175 g/6 oz Danish Blue cheese
3 red eating apples
juice of 1 lemon
French Dressing (see Tossed Green Salad,
 page 11)
lettuce
chopped green pepper and parsley

1. Cut ham into 1-cm/½-inch squares. Roll cheese into small balls. Dice apples, leaving peel on, and

dip in lemon juice to preserve their colour. Toss apples and ham in a well-flavoured French dressing.

2. Line a dish with lettuce leaves, and fill with cheese balls, ham and apple. Sprinkle with chopped green pepper and garnish with parsley. Serve with additional French dressing.

Cheese Salad

225 g/8 oz Gruyère cheese, diced
1 small green pepper, finely chopped
12 black olives, sliced
4 level tablespoons double cream
salt and freshly ground black pepper
2 bunches watercress
olive oil
lemon juice or wine vinegar

1. Combine diced Gruyère, finely chopped pepper, sliced olives and cream. Season to taste with salt and freshly ground black pepper. Toss well and allow to marinate for at least 1 hour.

2. To serve: toss prepared watercress in a dressing of 3 parts olive oil to 1 part lemon juice or wine vinegar. Place cheese salad mixture in centre. Serve immediately.

Autumn Salad

150 ml/¼ pint Mayonnaise (see page 91)
150 ml/¼ pint soured cream
1 level teaspoon Dijon mustard
salt and freshly ground black pepper
100 g/4 oz Swiss cheese, cut into thin strips
100 g/4 oz cooked ham, cut into thin strips
2 tart apples, cored and thinly sliced
lemon juice
lettuce leaves

1. Blend mayonnaise, soured cream and Dijon mustard and season with salt and freshly ground black pepper, to taste.

2. Combine cheese, ham and apple in a bowl. Pour over lemon juice and toss. Then add Soured

Cream Mayonnaise dressing and mix all together gently.

3. Serve on a bed of fresh lettuce.

Cucumber Salad Ring Mould

CUCUMBER RING MOULD
3 cucumbers
½ medium-sized onion
juice of 2 lemons
2 level teaspoons salt
freshly ground black pepper
2 level tablespoons gelatine
150 ml/¼ pint cold water
450 ml/¾ pint chicken stock
2 level teaspoons parsley
1 level teaspoon chopped tarragon
curly endive
well-flavoured French Dressing (see
    Tossed Green Salad, page 11)

GARNISH
12 black olives
3 ripe tomatoes, quartered
2 tablespoons finely chopped parsley or
    chervil

1. Remove peel from cucumbers and grate cucumber finely. Grate onion, strain lemon juice and mix together. Season with salt and freshly ground black pepper.

2. Soften gelatine in cold water. After about 5 minutes, pour in boiling stock and stir until dissolved. Cool; mix with cucumber mixture, and add finely chopped parsley and tarragon. Pour into a large ring mould or two smaller moulds. Chill until firm.

3. When ready to serve: turn out cucumber ring on a serving dish and fill centre with curly endive. Pour well-flavoured French dressing over salad. Garnish dish with olives and tomatoes and sprinkle with finely chopped parsley or chervil.

Note: The centre of the cucumber ring may also be filled with Mayonnaise of Chicken (see page 24) or Tuna Waldorf Salad (see page 33).

23

24

Mayonnaise of Chicken

6 level tablespoons stiff Mayonnaise
   (see page 91)
lemon juice
salt, celery salt and freshly ground black
   pepper
1 lettuce, finely shredded
3 hard-boiled eggs, finely chopped
350 g/12 oz cooked chicken, diced
4 sticks celery, diced
100 g/4 oz tuna fish, diced

1. Thin mayonnaise with lemon juice and season to taste with salt, celery salt and freshly ground black pepper.

2. Combine mayonnaise with shredded lettuce, finely chopped hard-boiled eggs, diced chicken, celery and tuna fish. Mix well. Add more lemon juice, mayonnaise and seasoning if desired.

Truffled Turkey Salad

8-10 level tablespoons stiff Mayonnaise (see
   page 91)
lemon juice
1 small can black truffles
salt, celery salt and freshly ground black
   pepper
1 lettuce, finely shredded
4 hard-boiled eggs, finely chopped
675 g/1½ lb cooked turkey, diced
4 sticks celery, thinly sliced
4 tablespoons olive oil

1. Thin mayonnaise with lemon juice and the juice from a small can of black truffles and season to taste with salt, celery salt and freshly ground black pepper.

2. Add 2 tablespoons finely sliced black truffles to mayonnaise, then combine with shredded lettuce, finely chopped eggs, diced turkey and sliced celery. Add olive oil and mix well. Add more lemon juice, mayonnaise and seasoning if desired.

Duck and Fresh Fruit Salad

675 g/1½ lb cold roast duck, cut into 'fingers'
2 oranges, peeled and cut into segments
2 thick slices fresh pineapple, peeled and cut
   into segments
8 peeled segments grapefruit
Soured Cream Mayonnaise (see Autumn
   Salad, page 23)
salt and freshly ground black pepper
crisp lettuce leaves
12 black olives
2 level tablespoons finely chopped chives,
   parsley or tarragon

1. Combine diced duck with segments of orange, pineapple and grapefruit. Add enough Soured Cream Mayonnaise to coat pieces lightly. Season with salt and freshly ground black pepper.

2. Arrange lettuce leaves around a shallow salad bowl. Pile duck and fruit mixture in centre of dish. Garnish with black olives and a sprinkling of finely chopped fresh herbs.

Duck and Orange Salad

diced meat of 1 roasted duck
4 shallots, finely chopped
2 sticks celery, sliced
olive oil and wine vinegar
salt and freshly ground black pepper
rosemary
4 small oranges, peeled and segmented
lettuce
8-10 black olives

1. Combine diced duck, finely chopped shallots and sliced celery with a dressing made of 3 parts olive oil to 1 part wine vinegar. Season to taste with salt, freshly ground black pepper and rosemary. Toss well. Allow duck to marinate in this mixture for at least 2 hours.

2. Just before serving, add orange segments, toss again, adding more dressing if required.

3. Line a glass salad bowl with lettuce leaves. Fill with salad and garnish with black olives.

Vinaigrette Sauce with variations

Garden Vegetables

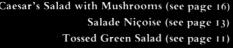
Caesar's Salad with Mushrooms (see page 16)
Salade Niçoise (see page 13)
Tossed Green Salad (see page 11)

Swedish Buffet Salad

1 kg/2 lb cold poached halibut
4 tart eating apples
2 level tablespoons butter
2 tablespoons cider
150 ml/¼ pint soured cream
2 level tablespoons grated horseradish
1 level tablespoon prepared mustard
2 tablespoons lemon juice
salt and freshly ground black pepper
2 hard-boiled eggs, finely chopped
sprigs of fresh watercress

1. Carefully flake poached halibut.

2. Peel, core and slice apples thinly.

3. Combine butter and cider in a frying pan and sauté apple slices until soft, stirring constantly.

4. Force apples and pan juices through a fine sieve and add soured cream, grated horseradish, prepared mustard and lemon juice.

5. Beat mixture until light and foamy, adding a little more cider if necessary, and toss flaked fish gently in this dressing. Season to taste with salt and freshly ground black pepper, and arrange salad in a glass serving bowl. Decorate with finely chopped hard-boiled egg and sprigs of fresh watercress.

Cold Lamb Salad

about 450 g/1 lb cold roast lamb
¼ Spanish onion, finely chopped
2 sticks celery, sliced
olive oil
tarragon vinegar
salt and freshly ground black pepper
1 level teaspoon finely chopped fresh
   tarragon
finely chopped parsley

1. Slice lamb thinly and then cut into thin strips.

2. Combine lamb with finely chopped onion and sliced celery in a salad bowl. Pour over a well-flavoured dressing made with olive oil and tarra-gon vinegar and season to taste with salt and freshly ground black pepper.

3. Just before serving, sprinkle with finely chopped tarragon and parsley.

French Bean and Prawn Salad

450 g/1 lb haricots verts
well-flavoured French Dressing (see Tossed
   Green Salad, page 11)
225 g/8 oz Norwegian prawns
2 level tablespoons finely chopped onion
lemon juice
cayenne
lettuce leaves
olive oil
salt and freshly ground black pepper
2 level tablespoons chopped parsley
2 level tablespoons chopped chives
1 small clove garlic, finely chopped

1. Top and tail young green beans and cook them in boiling salted water until they are barely tender. Drain and toss immediately while still warm in a well-flavoured French dressing. Chill.

2. Defrost prawns in a small bowl. Drain, add finely chopped onion, lemon juice and cayenne, to taste, and toss well. Chill.

3. When ready to serve: drain prawns and beans from their respective marinades. Combine in a shallow salad bowl, garnish with lettuce leaves and add olive oil, lemon juice and salt and freshly ground black pepper, to taste. Sprinkle with chopped parsley and chives and finely chopped garlic.

30

Champagne Prawn Bowl

450 g/1 lb cooked small new potatoes
225 g/8 oz cooked prawns, shelled
French Dressing (see Tossed Green Salad,
    page 11)
2 hard-boiled eggs, sliced
lettuce leaves
2 level tablespoons finely chopped fennel or
    tarragon

MARINADE
8 black olives, stoned and sliced
¼ bottle dry champagne
2 shallots, finely chopped
2 level tablespoons finely chopped parsley
1 clove garlic, finely chopped
salt and freshly ground black pepper

1. Peel and slice new potatoes. Add shelled cooked prawns with first 5 marinade ingredients and season with salt and freshly ground black pepper. Chill and marinate overnight.

2. One hour before serving: drain off juices and dress salad with a well-flavoured French dressing.

3. Line a salad bowl with lettuce leaves. Arrange tossed salad ingredients in the centre; top with sliced hard-boiled eggs and chopped fennel or tarragon and serve immediately.

Salade Emile

4 tomatoes
1 large green pepper
4 sticks celery, thinly sliced
2 hard-boiled eggs, quartered
16 anchovy fillets
1 (198-g/7-oz) can tuna fish
green and black olives
mustard-flavoured French Dressing (see
    Tossed Green Salad, page 11)
1 level tablespoon each finely chopped
    chives, chervil, parsley and tarragon

1. Peel tomatoes and cut into quarters. Seed pepper and slice very thinly. Combine tomatoes and pepper with sliced celery and quartered hard-boiled eggs.

2. Garnish salad with anchovies, tuna fish and green and black olives and pour over a mustard-flavoured French dressing to which you have added finely chopped chives, chervil, parsley and tarragon.

Fruit Salads

Roquefort Pear Salad

4 ripe pears
juice of 1 lemon
100 g/4 oz Roquefort cheese
150 ml/¼ pint double cream
1 tablespoon cognac
paprika
Cos lettuce leaves
French Dressing (see Tossed Green Salad,
   page 11)
halved walnuts

1. Peel and core pears. Cut into 5-mm/¼-inch slices. Marinate in lemon juice to keep from browning.

2. Combine Roquefort cheese, cream and cognac and mash to a smooth paste. Add lemon juice (from pears) and paprika, to taste.

3. Sandwich cheese mixture between pear slices. Place on a bed of Cos lettuce leaves and dress with French dressing. Garnish with halved walnuts.

Fruit Salad with Mint Dressing

1 grapefruit
2 oranges
2 apples
2 pears
1 small bunch grapes

MINT DRESSING
2 level tablespoons finely chopped mint
   leaves
1 level tablespoon finely chopped chives
150 ml/¼ pint well-flavoured French
   Dressing (see Tossed Green Salad,
   page 11)
sugar

1. Peel and dice grapefruit and oranges.

2. Core and dice apples and pears, but do not peel.

3. Halve and seed grapes.

4. **To make Mint Dressing:** add finely chopped mint and chives to well-flavoured French dressing. Sweeten to taste with a little sugar. Chill in refrigerator for at least 1 hour before using.

5. Combine fruits and toss with Mint Dressing.

Pear Waldorf Salad

6 ripe pears
juice of 1 lemon
6 sticks celery, sliced
50 g/2 oz halved walnuts
Mayonnaise (see page 91) or French
   Dressing (see Tossed Green Salad,
   page 11)
1 lettuce

1. Halve and core pears. Cut into cubes and sprinkle with lemon juice.

2. Add sliced celery and walnut halves.

3. Toss together in mayonnaise or French dressing according to taste, and pile into a salad bowl lined with lettuce leaves.

Greek Orange and Olive Salad

3-4 ripe oranges
10-12 large black olives
1-2 level tablespoons finely chopped onion
150 ml/¼ pint well-flavoured French
   Dressing (see Tossed Green Salad,
   page 11)
salt and freshly ground black pepper

1. Peel and thinly slice oranges crosswise. Cut slices into quarters.

2. Stone and slice olives.

3. Combine orange quarters and olives in a salad bowl with finely chopped onion and French dressing. Season with salt and freshly ground black pepper, and toss before serving.

32

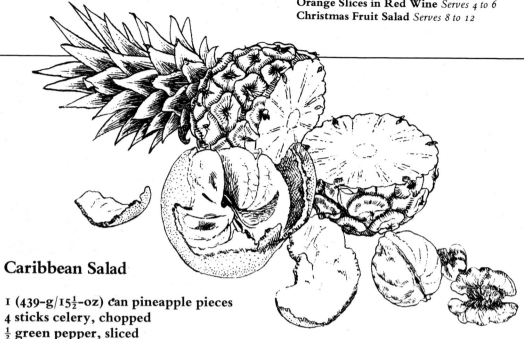

Caribbean Salad

I (439-g/15½-oz) can pineapple pieces
4 sticks celery, chopped
½ green pepper, sliced
½ red pepper, sliced
4-6 level tablespoons coarsely chopped
   walnuts
4-6 level tablespoons well-flavoured
   Mayonnaise (see page 91)
lemon juice
lettuce

1. Drain pineapple pieces, reserving juice, and combine with celery, peppers, walnuts and mayonnaise.

2. Moisten salad with lemon juice and reserved pineapple juice, to taste.

3. Arrange some lettuce leaves on individual salad plates and mound Caribbean Salad in the centre.

Orange Slices in Red Wine

225 g/8 oz sugar
150 ml/¼ pint water
red Burgundy
I clove
cinnamon
orange peel
lemon peel
4 large navel oranges

1. Make a syrup of sugar and water. Combine with 150 ml/¼ pint red Burgundy, clove, cin-

namon and 2 strips each of orange and lemon peel. Boil until syrupy and reduced. Add another 2 tablespoons red Burgundy.

2. Peel oranges. Divide into segments and remove all membrane and pith.

3. Place orange segments in warm syrup and chill in refrigerator. Serve with slivers of fresh orange peel.

Christmas Fruit Salad

1-2 lettuces
I bunch watercress
1-2 cloves garlic, finely chopped
2 level tablespoons finely chopped chives (or
   parsley)
olive oil
wine vinegar
coarse salt and freshly ground black pepper
4 slices pineapple, cut in thin wedges
2 oranges, peeled and cut in thin segments

1. Wash and prepare lettuce and watercress. Shake dry in a salad basket, or dry carefully in a clean tea towel.

2. Arrange lettuces and watercress in bowl. Combine finely chopped garlic and chives (or parsley). Sprinkle over the salad and dress with an olive oil and wine vinegar dressing (3 to 4 parts oil to 1 part vinegar). Season to taste with coarse salt and freshly ground black pepper.

3. Just before serving, toss salad until each leaf is glistening and garnish with pineapple wedges and orange segments.

Apple Coleslaw

350 g/12 oz crisp white cabbage, shredded
1 (226-g/8-oz) can pineapple cubes
2 tart eating apples, cored and sliced
2 sticks celery, finely sliced
150 ml/¼ pint Mayonnaise (see page 91)
lettuce

GARNISH
8 black olives, stoned
8 walnuts, coarsely chopped
parsley
1 tart eating apple, cored, sliced and dipped
   in lemon juice to preserve colour

1. Crisp cabbage in cold water for 30 minutes. Dry.

2. Combine crisped cabbage, drained pineapple chunks, sliced apples and celery with mayonnaise, tossing well until mayonnaise coats all ingredients.

3. Line salad bowl with lettuce leaves, pile salad in the centre and serve garnished with black olives, walnuts, parsley and sliced apple.

My Coleslaw

350 g/12 oz white cabbage, finely shredded
1 Spanish onion
2 red apples
1–2 tablespoons capers
1 dill-pickled cucumber, sliced thinly
well-flavoured French Dressing (see Tossed
   Green Salad, page 11)

1. Crisp cabbage in cold water for at least 30 minutes. Drain well and roll in a clean tea towel to dry.

2. Slice onion finely and separate into rings; core apples and cut into thin wedges.

3. Combine onion rings, apple wedges, drained cabbage, capers and pickled cucumber and toss with well-flavoured French dressing.

Waldorf Salad

2 eating apples, diced
lemon juice
4 sticks celery, sliced
6 level tablespoons broken walnuts
salt and freshly ground black pepper
Mayonnaise (see page 91)
soured cream
watercress

1. Sprinkle diced apples with lemon juice to preserve colour. Add sliced celery and broken walnuts. Season with salt and freshly ground black pepper, to taste.

2. Toss together in 4 to 6 level tablespoons each of mayonnaise and soured cream and pile into a salad bowl lined with watercress.

Tuna Waldorf Salad

2 (198-g/7-oz) cans tuna fish, drained
4–6 sticks celery, sliced
6–8 level tablespoons broken walnuts
Mayonnaise (see page 91)
lemon juice
salt and freshly ground black pepper
cayenne
3 tart apples, cored but unpeeled
crisp lettuce leaves

1. Break tuna into bite-sized pieces. Combine with celery, walnuts and enough mayonnaise to hold ingredients together. Season with lemon juice, salt, freshly ground black pepper and cayenne, to taste.

2. Cut apples into small cubes; toss them in lemon juice to preserve colour and stir into tuna mixture. Serve in crisp lettuce leaves to form cups.

Spanish Summer Soup Salad

6 large ripe tomatoes
½ Spanish onion, thinly sliced
½ green pepper, seeded and thinly sliced
½ cucumber, peeled and thinly sliced
1 clove garlic, finely chopped
salt, Tabasco and freshly ground black
   pepper
6 tablespoons olive oil
3 tablespoons lemon juice
300-450 ml/½-¾ pint chilled chicken
   consommé

GARNISH
2 tomatoes, peeled, seeded and diced
½ green pepper, seeded and diced
¼ cucumber, peeled, seeded and diced
1 avocado pear, peeled, stoned, diced and
   brushed with lemon juice to preserve
   colour
garlic croûtons made from 4 slices white
   bread, diced and sautéed until crisp and
   golden in butter and olive oil
4 level tablespoons finely chopped chives
   or parsley

1. Seed tomatoes and dice coarsely. Combine in a salad bowl with thinly sliced Spanish onion, green pepper and cucumber. Season to taste with finely chopped garlic, salt, Tabasco and freshly ground black pepper, and marinate in olive oil and lemon juice in the refrigerator for at least 30 minutes.

2. Just before serving, add chilled chicken consommé.

3. Garnish with a sprinkling of diced tomato, green pepper, cucumber, avocado pear, garlic *croûtons*, and finely chopped chives or parsley.

Chilled Avocado Soup

1.75 litres/3 pints well-flavoured chicken
   stock
4 ripe avocado pears
lemon juice
salt and white pepper
6 drops Tabasco
150 ml/¼ pint double cream

1. Chill stock thoroughly.

2. Peel and halve avocado pears and remove stones. Brush avocados generously on all sides with lemon juice as soon as you cut and peel them, to prevent discoloration.

3. Purée avocado halves with chilled stock until smooth, either in an electric blender, or by rubbing them together through a very fine sieve. Season to taste with salt and white pepper.

4. Add Tabasco and cream and blend thoroughly. Taste again for seasoning, adding a little more salt or Tabasco, if necessary, and lemon juice to taste.

Watercress Vichyssoise *Serves 4 to 6*
Green Vegetable Soup with Cucumber *Serves 4 to 6*
Watercress and Mushroom Consommé *Serves 4 to 6*
Vegetable Consommé *Serves 4 to 6*

35

Watercress Vichyssoise

6 potatoes, peeled and sliced
3 large leeks, sliced
1½ bunches watercress
1 ham bone (optional)
1.75 litres/3 pints chicken stock (made with
    a stock cube)
salt and freshly ground black pepper
double cream, chilled
sprigs of watercress, to garnish

1. Cook sliced vegetables and watercress with ham bone in stock until done.

2. Blend in an electric blender, or purée through a fine sieve. Season with salt and freshly ground black pepper, and chill.

3. Just before serving, add chilled cream, to taste. Serve with sprigs of watercress.

Green Vegetable Soup with Cucumber

1 (113-g/4-oz) packet frozen peas
1 (227-g/8-oz) packet frozen leaf spinach
1.4 litres/2½ pints chicken consommé
8 level tablespoons butter
½ cucumber, peeled and seeded
2 egg yolks
150 ml/¼ pint double cream
salt and freshly ground black pepper
finely chopped parsley

1. Defrost peas and spinach leaves and simmer half of them in 4 tablespoons each chicken consommé and butter until cooked through. Drain and purée in an electric blender or push through a fine sieve.

2. Peel and seed cucumber and cut flesh into pea-sized dice. Combine diced cucumber with remaining peas and spinach leaves in remaining butter and cook gently until tender.

3. Beat egg yolks in a large bowl, stir in cream and puréed vegetables. Pour in remaining chicken consommé, whisking continuously, until well mixed. Transfer to a clean saucepan and cook over a gentle heat, stirring, until green-tinted soup is smooth and thick. Do not let soup come to the boil, or it will curdle.

4. Just before serving, stir in cooked peas, spinach and diced cucumber. Season to taste with salt and freshly ground black pepper. Sprinkle with finely chopped parsley.

Watercress and Mushroom Consommé

1 bunch watercress
6-8 button mushrooms
900 ml-1.15 litres/1½-2 pints chicken stock
4-6 tablespoons port wine or Madeira
salt and freshly ground black pepper

1. Wash watercress and remove leaves from stems. Wash and trim mushrooms, slice thinly.

2. Bring chicken stock to the boil. Add watercress leaves and thinly sliced mushrooms and heat through. Add port or Madeira and salt and freshly ground black pepper, to taste. Serve immediately.

Vegetable Consommé

900 ml-1.15 litres/1½-2 pints beef consommé
4-6 sticks celery, thinly sliced
100 g/4 oz green beans, cut in 2.5-cm/1-inch
    segments
salt and freshly ground black pepper
2-4 level tablespoons chopped chives,
    or parsley

1. Bring beef consommé to the boil. Add thinly sliced celery and bean segments. Allow the soup to simmer gently for 20 minutes. Season with salt and freshly ground black pepper, to taste.

2. Add finely chopped fresh herbs and serve immediately.

36

Danish Cabbage Soup

1 cabbage (about 1 kg/2 lb)
1 Spanish onion
4 level tablespoons butter
1–2 level tablespoons brown sugar
900 ml/1½ pints beef stock
4–6 whole allspice
salt and freshly ground black pepper
1 (142-ml/5-fl oz) carton soured cream

1. Slice cabbage and onion thinly.

2. Melt butter in a saucepan, stir in brown sugar and simmer, stirring constantly, for 1 minute. Then add sliced vegetables and cook, stirring, until vegetables are lightly browned.

3. Add beef stock and allspice and salt and freshly ground black pepper, to taste. Simmer gently for 30 to 40 minutes, until cabbage is tender.

4. Stir in soured cream. Correct seasoning and serve immediately.

Carrot Vichyssoise 'Four Seasons'

5 potatoes, sliced
7 large carrots, sliced
2 large leeks, sliced
1 ham bone
1.4 litres/2½ pints chicken stock
1–2 level teaspoons sugar
1 level tablespoon salt
freshly ground black pepper
600 ml/1 pint double cream
raw carrot, cut in fine strips

1. Cook sliced vegetables and ham bone in stock until potatoes and carrots are tender.

2. Purée vegetables and stock in a blender, or push through a fine sieve.

3. Season to taste with sugar, salt and a pinch of freshly ground black pepper. Stir in cream, heat through – but do not allow to come to the boil.

4. Serve with a garnish of fine strips of raw carrot.

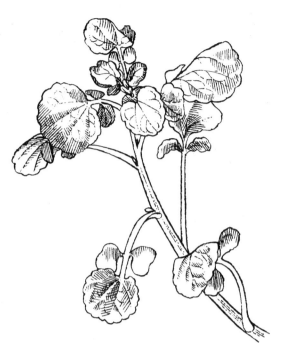

French Watercress Soup

4 level tablespoons butter
2 tablespoons olive oil
1 large onion, finely chopped
1 clove garlic, finely chopped
225 g/8 oz potatoes, peeled and thinly sliced
salt and freshly ground black pepper
1½ bunches watercress
300 ml/½ pint milk
300 ml/½ pint chicken stock
8–10 tablespoons single cream
2 egg yolks

1. Heat butter and olive oil until melted in a large, heavy saucepan. Sauté finely chopped onion and garlic over a moderate heat until transparent but not coloured.

2. Add sliced potatoes, sprinkle with salt and freshly ground black pepper and cover with 300 ml/½ pint water. Bring to the boil, reduce heat and simmer until potatoes are almost tender, 5 to 7 minutes.

3. Wash watercress carefully. Separate stems from leaves. Put about a quarter of the best leaves aside for garnish. Chop stalks coarsely and add them to the simmering pan, together with remaining leaves.

4. Stir in milk and chicken stock. Bring to the boil and simmer for 15 to 20 minutes, or until all the vegetables are very soft.

5. Rub soup through a fine wire sieve, or purée in an electric blender. Pour back into the rinsed-out saucepan, correct seasoning if necessary and reheat gently.

6. Blend cream with egg yolks. Pour into the heating soup and continue to cook, stirring constantly, until soup thickens slightly. Do not allow soup to boil once the egg yolks have been added, or they will scramble and ruin its appearance.

7. Shred reserved watercress leaves, sprinkle them over the soup and serve immediately.

Minestre Verde

Illustrated on page 48

225 g/8 oz dried haricot beans
4 rashers lean bacon
1 garlic clove
2.25 litres/2 quarts chicken stock
2 leeks
4-6 tomatoes
4 tablespoons olive oil
2 level tablespoons chopped herbs (parsley, basil, chives, oregano)
1 (100-g/4-oz) packet frozen peas
225 g/8 oz sliced green beans
1 potato, diced
salt and freshly ground black pepper
100-175 g/4-6 oz small elbow macaroni

GARNISH
2 level tablespoons finely chopped parsley
2 tablespoons olive oil
4-6 level tablespoons freshly grated Parmesan cheese

1. Place dried beans in a large saucepan, fill pan three-quarters full with cold water and bring to the boil. Remove pan from the heat and allow beans to stand in water for 1 hour.

2. Drain beans and put them in a large, clean saucepan with bacon and garlic and enough chicken stock (made with a cube) to cover. Simmer for $1\frac{1}{2}$ hours, adding more stock if necessary.

3. In the meantime, wash leeks carefully and chop. Peel and seed tomatoes and chop.

4. Sauté chopped leeks and tomatoes in olive oil until vegetables are soft. Add chopped herbs and cook for a few minutes more before adding peas, green beans and diced potato. Season with salt and freshly ground black pepper. Cook over a high heat for 10 minutes. Add reserved beans and their cooking liquid and elbow macaroni and cook until pasta is tender.

5. Stir in finely chopped parsley and olive oil. Sprinkle with grated Parmesan cheese.

Spanish Carrot Soup

675 g/$1\frac{1}{2}$ lb carrots
softened butter
6-8 tablespoons dry sherry
900 ml/$1\frac{1}{2}$ pints well-flavoured chicken stock
salt and freshly ground black pepper
2 egg yolks
300 ml/$\frac{1}{2}$ pint double cream

1. Peel carrots and cut into 1-cm/$\frac{1}{2}$-inch slices.

2. Heat 2 level tablespoons softened butter and cook carrots until golden, stirring frequently. Do not allow to scorch. Add 4 tablespoons dry sherry and 300 ml/$\frac{1}{2}$ pint chicken stock and bring to the boil. Reduce heat and simmer, covered, until the carrots are tender. Remove from the heat. Purée.

3. Return carrot purée to the heat, stir in 2 level tablespoons butter and remaining chicken stock, season with salt and freshly ground black pepper and simmer until heated through.

4. In another pan, melt 2 level tablespoons butter, beat in the egg yolks and double cream and add to the soup. Heat through, but do not allow soup to come to the boil. Just before serving, stir in 2 or more tablespoons dry sherry.

38

Prawn and Corn Chowder
Illustrated on page 48

1 (198-g/7-oz) can corn niblets
100 g/4 oz frozen Norwegian prawns
½ Spanish onion, finely chopped
2 level tablespoons butter
2.25 litres/4 pints chicken stock
freshly ground black pepper
1-2 tablespoons soy sauce
2 eggs, beaten
2-4 level tablespoons freshly chopped
    parsley

1. Drain corn niblets. Defrost prawns.

2. Sauté chopped onion in butter until soft; add chicken stock and corn niblets and simmer gently for 20 minutes. Then add prawns and continue to simmer for 10 more minutes.

3. Just before serving, add freshly ground black pepper and soy sauce to taste. Beat in eggs, sprinkle with chopped parsley and serve immediately.

Cream of Potato Soup

2 large Spanish onions
4 level tablespoons butter
6 medium potatoes
900 ml/1½ pints chicken stock
salt, freshly ground black pepper and nutmeg
300 ml/½ pint double cream
finely chopped chives

1. Peel onions and slice thinly. Sauté the onion rings gently in butter until soft. Do not allow to brown.

2. Peel and slice potatoes and add to onions with chicken stock, and salt, freshly ground black pepper and finely grated nutmeg, to taste, and simmer until vegetables are cooked.

3. Push the vegetables and stock through a wire sieve, or blend in an electric blender until smooth.

4. Just before serving, add cream and heat

through without boiling. Serve immediately sprinkled with chives.

Broccoli Cream Soup

2 (283-g/10-oz) packets frozen broccoli
1 stick celery, thinly sliced
1 small onion, thinly sliced
900 ml/1½ pints boiling chicken stock
generous pinch ground cloves
salt and freshly ground black pepper
about 300 ml/½ pint single cream

GARNISH
thin lemon slices
lightly salted whipped cream

1. Bring vegetables to boil in stock and simmer until tender.

2. Purée in electric blender or *mouli* or rub through fine sieve.

3. Add cloves, seasoning and thin with cream. Reheat, stirring, without boiling. Garnish with lemon slices topped with salted whipped cream.

Cream of Spinach Soup

1 kg/2 lb fresh spinach leaves
4 level tablespoons butter
salt and freshly ground black pepper
nutmeg
300 ml/½ pint double cream
600 ml/1 pint chicken stock (made with a
    cube)
finely chopped parsley
croûtons of fried diced bread

1. Wash the spinach leaves, changing water several times. Drain them thoroughly.

2. Put spinach in a thick-bottomed saucepan with butter, and cook gently, stirring continuously, until spinach is soft and tender.

3. Blend in an electric blender, or put through a

wire sieve. Season generously with salt, freshly ground black pepper and nutmeg.

4. Combine purée with cream and chicken stock, and heat through. Sprinkle with finely chopped parsley and fried diced bread. Serve immediately.

Cream of Onion Soup

6 Spanish onions
4 level tablespoons butter
sugar
600 ml/1 pint chicken stock (made with a
   cube)
300 ml/½ pint milk
2 tablespoons Cognac
½ level tablespoon Dijon mustard
300 ml/½ pint double cream
salt and freshly ground black pepper
nutmeg
croûtons made from 2 slices bread, diced
   and sautéed in butter until crisp and
   golden

1. Peel and slice onions thinly.

2. Heat butter in a large saucepan with a little sugar. Add the onion rings and cook them very, very gently over a low heat, stirring constantly with a wooden spoon, until the rings are just beginning to turn colour. Add chicken stock and milk gradually, stirring constantly until the soup begins to boil. Then lower the heat, cover the pan, and simmer gently until onions are soft.

3. Blend to a smooth purée in an electric blender. Add cognac, mustard and double cream and season to taste with salt, freshly ground black pepper and nutmeg and heat through.

4. Pour soup into individual soup bowls. Sprinkle with *croûtons* and serve immediately.

Vegetable Appetisers

Leeks à la Vinaigrette *Serves 4*
Herbed Carrots Vinaigrette *Serves 4*
Brussels Sprouts à la Vinaigrette *Serves 4*
Italian Pepper Salad *Serves 6*

40

Leeks à la Vinaigrette

12 small or 8 large leeks
salt
6-8 tablespoons olive oil
2 tablespoons wine vinegar
freshly ground black pepper and
    mustard
finely chopped parsley

1. Trim roots and cut off the tops of leeks, leaving 2.5 cm/1 inch to 7.5 cm/3 inches of the green portion. Halve the leeks, leaving the halves attached at the root end. Wash thoroughly.

2. Simmer leeks in boiling salted water for 20 minutes, or until tender. Drain thoroughly.

3. Arrange leeks in an *hors-d'oeuvre* dish.

4. Combine olive oil and vinegar with salt, freshly ground black pepper and mustard, to taste. Pour over leeks and garnish with finely chopped parsley.

Herbed Carrots Vinaigrette

450 g/1 lb new carrots
4 level tablespoons butter
4 tablespoons chicken stock
sugar
salt and freshly ground black pepper
2 level tablespoons each chopped parsley
    and chervil
well-flavoured French Dressing (see Tossed
    Green Salad, page 11)

1. Wash carrots and cut diagonally into thin slices.

2. Place prepared carrots in a saucepan of cold water, bring to the boil and drain.

3. Simmer carrots for 15 to 20 minutes in butter and chicken stock, with sugar, salt and freshly ground black pepper, to taste. Cool.

4. Just before serving sprinkle with chopped parsley and chervil and toss in French dressing.

Brussels Sprouts à la Vinaigrette

450 g/1 lb small Brussels sprouts
salt and freshly ground black pepper
6 tablespoons olive oil
grated rind and juice of $\frac{1}{2}$ lemon
2 tablespoons finely chopped chives
2 tablespoons finely chopped parsley
2 tablespoons chopped hard-boiled egg

1. **To prepare Brussels sprouts:** cut off stem ends and remove any wilted or damaged outer leaves from small Brussels sprouts. (If Brussels sprouts are older, remove tough outer leaves entirely.) Soak sprouts in cold water with a little salt or lemon juice for 15 minutes.

2. **To cook Brussels sprouts:** add sprouts to boiling salted water and simmer, uncovered, for 5 minutes. Cover pan and continue to cook for 7 (if very young) to 15 minutes longer, until just tender. Drain well and season generously with salt and freshly ground black pepper.

3. Place sprouts in a salad bowl. Add olive oil and lemon juice and toss well. Season with salt and freshly ground black pepper, add grated lemon rind and toss again.

4. Just before serving, sprinkle with finely chopped chives, parsley and hard-boiled egg.

Italian Pepper Salad

900 g/2 lb large, firm peppers (green, red
    and yellow)
150 ml/$\frac{1}{4}$ pint olive oil
2 cloves garlic, finely chopped
lemon juice
salt and freshly ground black pepper

1. Place peppers under the grill as close to the heat as possible, turning them from time to time until the skin is charred on all sides. Then rub the charred skins off under running water. Remove stems and seeds.

2. Cut lengthwise into 2.5-cm/1-inch strips. Rinse well and drain.

3. Place peppers in a salad bowl with olive oil and finely chopped garlic. Add lemon juice, salt and freshly ground black pepper, to taste. Chill for at least 1 hour before serving.

Mushroom and Bacon Hors-d'Oeuvre

450 g/1 lb button mushrooms
2 tablespoons lemon juice
225 g/8 oz green bacon, in 1 piece
2 tablespoons butter
2 tablespoons olive oil
½ Spanish onion, finely chopped
freshly ground black pepper
½ wine glass dry white wine
beurre manié (made by mashing 1
   tablespoon butter with 1 tablespoon flour
   to a smooth paste)
finely chopped parsley

1. Wash mushrooms, trim stalks and cut into quarters. Soak in a bowl of water with lemon juice until ready to use.

2. Dice green bacon.

3. Heat butter and olive oil in a large, thick-bottomed frying pan. Sauté finely chopped onion and diced green bacon in this until onion is transparent. Season to taste with freshly ground black pepper. Add quartered mushrooms and dry white wine and continue cooking over a low heat until mushrooms are tender but not soft. Stir in *beurre manié* and cook for a minute or two more, until sauce is thick. Serve, sprinkled with finely chopped parsley, in individual ramekins or little soufflé dishes.

Artichokes with Walnut Oil Dressing

4 artichokes
salt
juice of ½ lemon
freshly ground black pepper
finely chopped fresh herbs

WALNUT OIL DRESSING
150 ml/¼ pint double cream
salt and freshly ground black pepper
walnut oil
lemon juice

1. Remove the tough outer leaves of artichokes and trim tops of inner leaves. Trim the base and stem of each artichoke with a sharp knife. Cook until tender (30 to 40 minutes) in a large quantity of boiling salted water to which you have added the juice of ½ lemon. Artichokes are cooked when a leaf pulls out easily.

2. Turn artichokes upside down to drain.

3. Remove inner leaves of cooked artichokes, leaving a decorative outer ring of 2 or 3 leaves to form a cup around the heart of each artichoke. With the point of a spoon, remove choke from each artichoke. Season with salt and freshly ground black pepper and chill in the refrigerator.

4. To make Walnut Oil Dressing: whip double cream until stiff; flavour with salt, freshly ground black pepper and walnut oil and lemon juice, to taste.

5. Just before serving: pile artichoke hearts with whipped walnut cream filling and sprinkle with finely chopped herbs.

42

Choucroute Froide

1 Spanish onion, finely chopped
8 tablespoons olive oil
450 g/1 lb sauerkraut
300 ml/½ pint chicken stock
salt and coarsely ground black pepper
1 clove garlic, finely chopped
2 tablespoons wine vinegar
2 hard-boiled eggs, quartered
1 beetroot, cooked and sliced

1. Sauté finely chopped onion in 2 tablespoons olive oil until golden but not brown.

2. Place sauerkraut and onion in a heavy saucepan, and pour chicken stock over them. Simmer for 45 minutes.

3. Cool sauerkraut. Season to taste with salt and coarsely ground black pepper, and mix finely chopped garlic, remaining olive oil and the vinegar.

4. Serve garnished with quartered hard-boiled eggs and thin slices of cooked beetroot.

Cold Aubergine and Tomato Appetiser

4 aubergines
salt
6-8 ripe tomatoes
2 Spanish onions
freshly ground black pepper
olive oil

1. Peel aubergines and slice thinly. Sprinkle with salt and place slices under a weight for 30 minutes. Rinse thoroughly with cold water, drain and dry. Slice tomatoes and onions thinly. Keep separate.

2. Arrange a thin layer of onion slices in the bottom of a shallow baking dish, then a layer of aubergine slices, then one of tomato slices. Season with freshly ground black pepper. Repeat until all the vegetables are used up, ending with a layer of onion. Pour in olive oil until vegetables are barely covered. Bake in a very cool oven (120°C, 250°F, Gas Mark ½) for about 3 hours, or until vegetables are cooked through. Chill and serve.

Vegetable Antipasto
Illustrated on page 48

2 courgettes
2 sticks celery
100 g/4 oz French beans
2 carrots
100 g/4 oz button mushrooms
6 small white onions
½ cauliflower
1 green pepper
1 red pepper
1 small aubergine
8 tablespoons olive oil
1 clove garlic, chopped
1-2 bay leaves
8 tablespoons tomato ketchup
4 tablespoons wine vinegar
2 tablespoons granulated sugar
2 level tablespoons prepared mustard
salt and freshly ground black pepper
lettuce leaves
finely chopped parsley

1. Cut the courgettes into 5-mm/¼-inch slices. Cut the celery into 2.5-cm/1-inch pieces. Slice the French beans into 2.5-cm/1-inch pieces. Scrape carrots and cut into 2.5-cm/1-inch pieces. Wipe the mushrooms with a damp towel and quarter. Cut the onions into quarters. Trim the cauliflower and break into small flowerets. Remove pith and seeds from the green and red peppers and cut into strips. Cut the unpeeled aubergine into small cubes.

2. Heat the olive oil in a large, heavy skillet. Add chopped garlic and sauté until golden. Remove garlic and discard. Add the bay leaves and all the vegetables and cook over medium heat until tender but still slightly crisp.

3. Stir in the tomato ketchup, wine vinegar, sugar, mustard and salt and freshly ground black pepper, to taste, and cook for another 5 minutes.

4. Cool and then chill in the refrigerator. Just before serving, correct seasoning with additional mustard, salt and freshly ground black pepper, if desired. The important thing to remember when preparing this dish is to observe the undercooking rule. All the vegetables should be *al dente*.

5. **To serve:** place vegetables on lettuce leaves and sprinkle with finely chopped parsley.

Devilled Carrot Appetiser

1 kg/2 lb small carrots
1 clove garlic, finely chopped
½ Spanish onion, finely chopped
6 tablespoons olive oil
6 tablespoons water
1 tablespoon wine vinegar
1 level tablespoon dry mustard
¼ level tablespoon powdered cumin
¼ level tablespoon paprika
¼ level tablespoon cayenne
salt and freshly ground black pepper
2 level tablespoons chopped parsley
lemon juice

1. Peel and slice carrots.

2. Sauté finely chopped garlic and onion in olive oil, stirring constantly, until vegetables are soft. Add sliced carrots and continue to cook, stirring for 2 minutes.

3. Add water, wine vinegar, spices, and salt and freshly ground black pepper, to taste, and simmer gently until carrots are tender.

4. Allow to cool. Sprinkle with finely chopped parsley and a little lemon juice just before serving.

43

44

Aubergine Omelette

1 medium-sized aubergine
salt
seasoned flour
olive oil
8-10 eggs
freshly ground black pepper
1 tablespoon water
2 level tablespoons butter

1. Wash aubergine, trim ends, and cut into 5-mm/ ¼-inch slices. Cut each slice into thin strips. Salt the strips and leave to sweat for 1 hour in a colander.

2. Rinse strips in cold water and squeeze them dry in a cloth. Toss aubergine strips in seasoned flour.

3. Heat 2 tablespoons olive oil in a frying pan and cook the strips until golden. Drain on absorbent paper. Keep warm.

4. Break eggs into a bowl and season to taste with salt and freshly ground black pepper.

5. Add water to eggs and beat with a fork or wire whisk just enough to mix yolks and whites.

6. Heat the omelette pan gradually on a medium heat until it is hot enough to make butter sizzle on contact.

7. Add 2 tablespoons olive oil and butter to heated pan and shake until butter is melted. When fat is sizzling, pour in the beaten eggs all at once. Quickly stir eggs for a second or two in the pan to assure even cooking just as you would for scrambled eggs. As omelette begins to set, add aubergine strips. Remove omelette from heat and, with one movement, slide the omelette towards the handle. When a third of the omelette has slid up the rounded edge of the pan, fold this quickly towards the centre with your palette knife. Raise the handle of the pan and slide opposite edge of omelette one-third up the side farthest away from the handle. Hold a heated serving dish under the pan, and, as the rim of the omelette touches the dish, raise the handle more

and more until the pan is turned upside down and your oval-shaped, lightly browned omelette rests on the dish. Pick up a small piece of butter on the point of a sharp knife and rub it over omelette. Serve immediately.

Italian Green Pepper Omelette

3 large green peppers
olive oil
salt and freshly ground black pepper
2 small cloves garlic, finely chopped
2 level tablespoons finely chopped parsley
8-10 eggs
1 tablespoon water
butter

1. Place green peppers in an ovenproof baking dish and bake them in a hot oven (230°C, 450°F, Gas Mark 8) for 20 to 30 minutes. Remove from oven and cover dish with a damp cloth for 10 minutes. Then, while peppers are still warm, remove skins carefully and cut peppers in halves. Scoop out seeds without damaging tender flesh of peppers. Cool and drain in a colander.

2. Cut peppers into strips and place in a shallow bowl. Add 3 tablespoons olive oil and season generously with salt and freshly ground black pepper. Sprinkle with finely chopped garlic and parsley and leave pepper strips to marinate in this mixture for at least 2 hours. Drain.

3. Break eggs into a bowl; season to taste with salt and freshly ground black pepper.

4. Prepare omelette as in Steps **5. 6.** and **7.** of Aubergine Omelette recipe (above), substituting green pepper strips for aubergine.

Hot Cauliflower Mousse (see page 49)

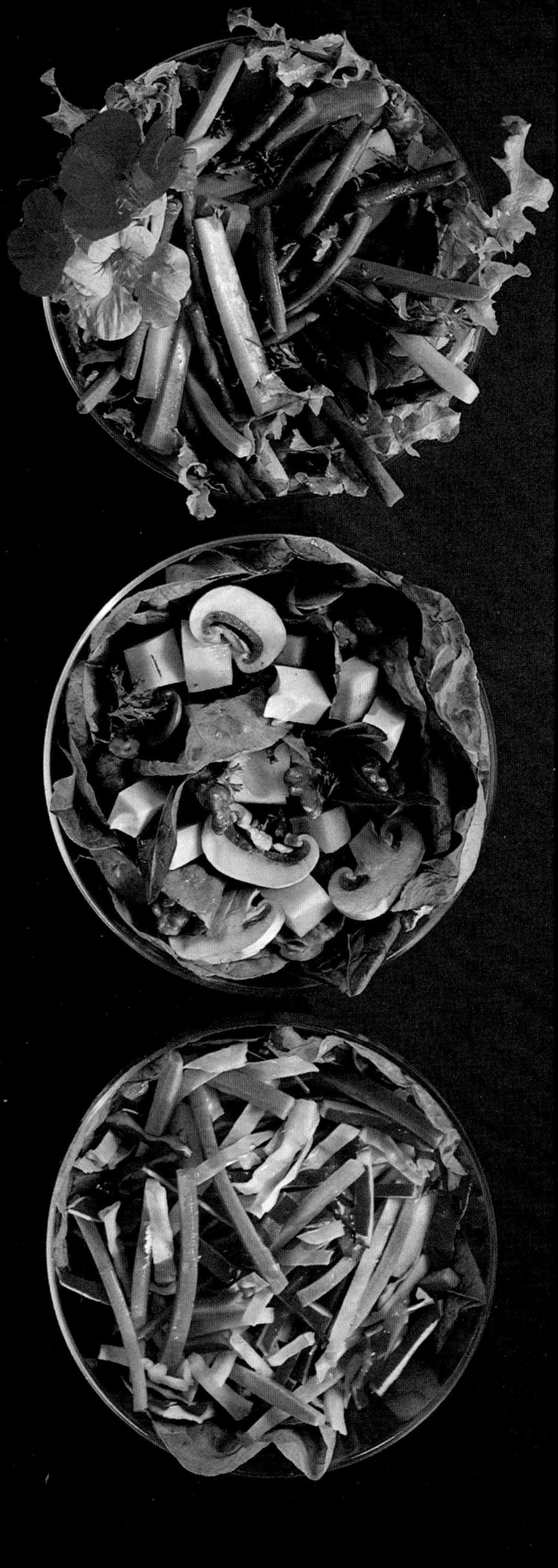

Prawn and Corn Chowder (see page 38)

Minestre Verde (see page 37)

Vegetable Antipasto (see page 43)

Red Pepper Omelette

4 tablespoons olive oil
½ Spanish onion, coarsely sliced
4 peppers (green, yellow and red), coarsely
    sliced
4 tomatoes, peeled and seeded
salt and freshly ground black pepper
8–10 eggs
2–4 level tablespoons freshly grated Gruyère
    cheese
2–4 level tablespoons freshly grated
    Parmesan cheese
2–4 level tablespoons butter

1. Heat olive oil in frying pan, add sliced onion and sauté, stirring from time to time, until onion is transparent. Add sliced and seeded peppers and cook over a low flame, stirring from time to time, until peppers are soft but not mushy.

2. Turn flame higher and stir in peeled and seeded tomatoes. Season generously with salt and freshly ground black pepper.

3. Break eggs into a bowl and beat with a whisk until foamy.

4. Pour eggs over vegetables, allow to set for a moment, then stir with a wooden spoon or spatula as you would for scrambled eggs. Sprinkle with finely grated cheese (Gruyère and Parmesan mixed) to bind mixture, and fold omelette into shape. Slide butter under omelette to add flavour, turn out on to a hot serving dish and serve immediately.

Hot Cauliflower Mousse

Illustrated on page 45

1 large cauliflower
salt
3 eggs
1 egg yolk
150 ml/¼ pint double cream
freshly ground black pepper
grated nutmeg
butter

GARNISH
**flowerets of cauliflower, poached
sprigs of fresh parsley or watercress
Hollandaise Sauce (see page 89)**

1. Clean cauliflower and cut into quarters. Cook in boiling salted water until just tender. Drain.

2. Preheat oven to moderate (180°C, 350°F, Gas Mark 4).

3. Put cooked cauliflower in the bowl of blender or food processor. Add eggs, egg yolk and cream. Season generously with salt, freshly ground black pepper and grated nutmeg. Put on lid of blender and blend until smooth.

4. Transfer mixture to a well-buttered soufflé dish with a band of aluminium foil tied around it, or a deep charlotte mould, and place in a roasting tin half full of boiling water on top of the cooker. Bring water to the boil again; then place the roasting tin in preheated oven and bake for 45 to 50 minutes, or until set.

5. Unmould mousse onto a heated serving dish. Garnish with sprigs of poached cauliflower and sprigs of parsley or watercress. Mask mousse with Hollandaise Sauce.

49

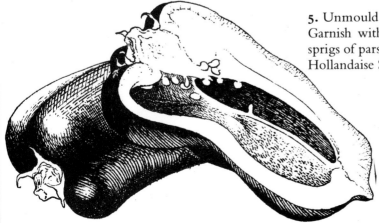

Cooked Vegetables

Basic Boiled Green Beans

450 g/1 lb green beans
salt and freshly ground black pepper
butter
2 level tablespoons finely chopped parsley

1. Cook beans in boiling salted water until tender – about 20 minutes.

2. Drain. Place in a heated serving dish. Season to taste with salt and freshly ground black pepper. Toss, sprinkle with lemon juice, to taste, and top with a piece of butter and finely chopped parsley.

Basic Steamed Green Beans

450 g/1 lb green beans
2 level tablespoons finely chopped shallots
   or spring onions
butter
lemon juice
salt and freshly ground black pepper

1. Place whole beans in a shallow *gratin* dish or bowl with finely chopped shallots or spring onions and 2 level tablespoons butter, and steam over boiling water in a tightly closed saucepan or double steamer until tender – 15 to 20 minutes.

2. Season to taste with lemon juice, salt and freshly ground black pepper. Toss, and top with a piece of butter.

Haricots Verts au Gratin

675 g/1½ lb thin haricots verts
salt
butter
450 ml/¾ pint double cream
freshly ground black pepper
4-6 level tablespoons freshly grated Gruyère
   cheese
2-4 level tablespoons freshly grated
   Parmesan cheese

1. Poach beans in salted water for 20 minutes, or until almost tender. Drain.

2. Place in a well-buttered *gratin* dish and cover with cream. Season to taste with salt and freshly ground black pepper, and place in a hot oven (230°C, 450°F, Gas Mark 8) for 20 minutes.

3. Sprinkle with freshly grated cheeses, dot with butter and return to the oven until the cheese is golden brown and bubbling.

Italian Green Beans

6 tablespoons chicken stock
2 tablespoons olive oil
4 canned Italian peeled tomatoes, diced
450 g/1 lb fresh green beans
salt and freshly ground black pepper
pinch of dried oregano (optional)
2 level tablespoons finely chopped parsley

1. Combine chicken stock, olive oil and diced tomatoes in a saucepan, and bring to the boil.

2. Add prepared green beans, season to taste with salt and freshly ground black pepper, and a pinch of oregano if desired. Cover saucepan and simmer gently for 1 hour.

3. Remove cover and continue to simmer until excess moisture has evaporated and beans are tender. Sprinkle with finely chopped parsley and serve.

Italian Green Beans with Ham

1 kg/2 lb green beans
salt
100 g/4 oz prosciutto (Parma ham)
2-4 level tablespoons butter
freshly ground black pepper
2 level tablespoons finely chopped parsley
1-2 cloves garlic, finely chopped

1. Top and tail beans and cook in boiling salted water until tender. The beans should remain firm. Drain.

2. Cut ham into thin strips. Melt butter in a frying pan and sauté ham for 2 to 3 minutes.

Green Beans à la Grecque *Serves 4*
French Green Beans with Almonds *Serves 4*
Creole Green Beans *Serves 6*

51

Add the drained beans and salt and freshly ground black pepper. Heat through.

3. Garnish with a sprinkling of finely chopped parsley and garlic and serve immediately.

Green Beans à la Grecque

450 g/1 lb green beans
1 (64-g/2¼-oz) can tomato purée
600 ml/1 pint water
4-6 tablespoons olive oil
½ Spanish onion, finely chopped
½ clove garlic, finely chopped
salt and freshly ground black pepper

1. Top and tail green beans, and slice them in half lengthwise.

2. Mix tomato purée with water, olive oil, and finely chopped onion and garlic.

3. Put beans in a saucepan; pour over tomato-

onion mixture, and season to taste with salt and freshly ground black pepper. Bring to the boil. Lower heat and simmer gently, stirring from time to time, for 45 minutes or until sauce has reduced and beans are tender.

French Green Beans with Almonds

1 kg/2 lb green beans
salt
2-4 level tablespoons butter
50 g/2 oz almonds, blanched and shredded
1 clove garlic, finely chopped
freshly ground black pepper

1. Top and tail beans and cook in boiling salted water until tender but still firm. Drain.

2. Melt butter in a frying pan and sauté almonds until golden. Add finely chopped garlic and cook for a second or two more.

3. Toss cooked beans with almonds and garlic until heated through. Season with salt and freshly ground black pepper, to taste; serve immediately.

Creole Green Beans

1 kg/2 lb green beans
salt
2 level tablespoons finely chopped onion
2 level tablespoons finely chopped green
   pepper
4 level tablespoons butter
4 level tablespoons tomato ketchup
4 tablespoons vinegar
1 level tablespoon prepared mustard
1 level tablespoon curry powder
freshly ground black pepper

1. Top and tail beans and cook in boiling salted water until tender but still firm. Drain.

2. Sauté finely chopped onion and green pepper in butter until onion is transparent. Add all the remaining ingredients except cooked beans and simmer for 5 minutes. Add beans and cook over a low heat until beans are well flavoured.

52

Chinese Green Beans

450 g/1 lb green beans
2 tablespoons peanut oil or lard
1 level teaspoon salt
150 ml/¼ pint water
1 tablespoon soy sauce, sake or dry sherry

1. Wash and trim beans. Break them into sections about 2.5 cm/1 inch long.

2. Heat oil or lard in a *wok* or frying pan. Add beans and cook over medium heat for 1 minute, stirring constantly.

3. Add salt and water, cover pan and cook beans for 3 minutes. Remove cover and simmer, stirring from time to time, until all the water has evaporated – about 5 minutes. Add soy sauce, *sake* or dry sherry, to taste, and serve.

Purée of Green Beans

450 g/1 lb green beans
salt
4 level tablespoons double cream
freshly ground black pepper
freshly grated nutmeg

Use an electric blender for a particularly smooth purée. You can bind the purée with a little butter instead of cream, or it is excellent cold, mixed with a little well-flavoured mayonnaise.

1. Trim beans, wash them and drain well.

2. Bring a pan of water to the boil. When it begins to bubble, add a generous pinch of salt and the beans. Boil briskly for 30 minutes, or until very tender. Drain thoroughly.

3. Purée beans through a fine sieve and return to the pan. Reheat over a moderate heat, beating vigorously with a wooden spoon to evaporate excess moisture.

4. Add cream, mix well and season to taste with salt, freshly ground black pepper and a pinch of freshly grated nutmeg.

5. Spoon into a heated serving dish and serve immediately.

Soufflé of Green Beans

450 g/1 lb green beans
salt
butter
2 level tablespoons flour
300 ml/½ pint hot milk
freshly ground black pepper
4-6 level tablespoons grated Parmesan
   cheese
2 eggs, separated

1. Cook beans in boiling salted water until tender – about 20 minutes. Drain.

2. Place 2 level tablespoons butter in the top of a double saucepan and melt it over water. Stir in flour until smooth, add hot milk and cook over a low heat, stirring constantly, for 10 minutes. Season to taste with salt and freshly ground black pepper. Remove from heat and stir in cheese and egg yolks.

3. Sauté drained beans in frying pan with 2 tablespoons butter for about 3 minutes. Put through fine sieve, or blend in electric blender, and stir purée into sauce. Beat egg whites with a little salt until stiff. Fold into mixture.

4. Spoon into a well-buttered baking dish (or soufflé dish) and bake in a moderate oven (180°C, 350°F, Gas Mark 4) for 30 to 35 minutes. Serve immediately as a vegetable.

Frijoles – Mexican Fried Beans

450 g/1 lb red beans
salt
6 level tablespoons lard

1. Soak beans overnight.

2. Drain. Add water to cover, season to taste with salt, and cook slowly until very tender.

3. Drain the beans and mash them. Add very hot lard, and continue cooking, stirring from time to time, until fat is absorbed by the beans. Do not let fried beans scorch.

Note: the famous *frijoles refritos*, Mexican refried beans, are made by heating fat in frying pan, adding mashed fried beans, and cooking, stirring continuously, until beans are completely dry.

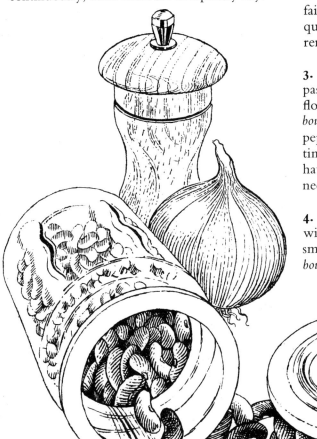

Kidney Beans in Red Wine

53

450 g/1 lb red kidney beans
1 Spanish onion
salt
butter
1 level tablespoon flour
1 bouquet garni (2 sprigs parsley, 2 sprigs thyme, 1 stalk celery, 1 bay leaf)
freshly ground black pepper
225 g/8 oz fat bacon, diced
150–300 ml/$\frac{1}{4}$–$\frac{1}{2}$ pint red wine

1. Place kidney beans in a large saucepan. Fill pan with water and bring gently to the boil. Then let beans soak off the heat for 1 hour.

2. Drain. Simmer with onion in salted water in a large casserole until beans are almost cooked through – 45 to 60 minutes. Beans should remain fairly firm, otherwise they will break in subsequent cooking. Drain beans, reserving liquid, and remove onion.

3. Mix 1 tablespoon butter and flour to a smooth paste. Combine drained beans with butter and flour in a saucepan. Add 150 ml/$\frac{1}{4}$ pint bean liquor, *bouquet garni*, and salt and freshly ground black pepper, to taste. Simmer, stirring gently from time to time, for about 10 minutes, or until beans have absorbed flavour, adding more liquor if necessary.

4. Sauté diced bacon until golden. Add to beans with red wine, and simmer gently until sauce is smooth and rich – about 30 minutes. Remove *bouquet garni*. Serve immediately.

Sautéed Bean Sprouts with Green Pepper *Serves 4*
Sautéed Bean Sprouts and Green Pepper with
   Chinese Pork or Duck *Serves 2 to 3 as a main dish*
Harvard Beets *Serves 4 to 6*
Orange Beetroot *Serves 4*

Bean Sprouts

Bean Sprouts – *tou ya ts'ai* in Chinese, *moyashi* in Japanese – grown from mung or soy beans, are sold fresh or canned in Chinese supermarkets. Fresh bean sprouts should be rinsed in a large bowl of cold water and carefully picked over to remove any sprouts that are discoloured or bruised. Chinese cooks always remove heads and tails of sprouts before using. Use bean sprouts the day they are bought for best results or keep for two or three days in the refrigerator in a plastic bag. Canned bean sprouts should be drained and rinsed before using.

Sautéed Bean Sprouts with Green Pepper

450 g/1 lb bean sprouts
1 green pepper
4 tablespoons peanut oil
½ level teaspoon sugar
2 tablespoons sake, dry white wine or dry
   sherry
1 tablespoon light soy sauce

1. Remove heads and tails of bean sprouts and soak sprouts in cold water. Drain.

2. Wash green pepper; remove stem and seeds and cut into threadlike lengths the same size as bean sprouts.

3. Heat oil in a Chinese *wok,* or frying pan, and sauté shredded green pepper for 2 minutes. Add sugar and drained bean sprouts and continue to cook, tossing vegetables continuously, for a minute or two more. Then add *sake* (or dry white wine or dry sherry) and soy sauce.

Sautéed Bean Sprouts and Green Pepper with Chinese Pork or Duck

Cut 175 g/6 oz cooked pork or duck into thin strips the size of the bean sprouts. Sauté meat in a little peanut oil until golden. Flavour with a hint of *sake* and light soy sauce and toss with bean sprouts and green pepper cooked as above.

Harvard Beets

1 (361-g/12¾-oz) jar baby beetroot
1 level tablespoon cornflour
3 tablespoons vinegar or lemon juice
2 level tablespoons sugar
salt and freshly ground black pepper
2 level tablespoons softened butter

1. Drain beetroot, reserving juice, and cut into even slices.

2. Mix cornflour with 150 ml/¼ pint reserved beet juice. Add vinegar (or lemon juice), sugar, and salt and freshly ground black pepper, to taste. Cook until thickened, stirring constantly.

3. Add sliced beetroot. Warm through.

4. Just before serving, add softened butter and simmer until it has melted. Correct seasoning, adding more vinegar (or lemon juice), sugar or salt, as needed.

Orange Beetroot

1 large cooked beetroot
1 level teaspoon grated orange rind
150 ml/¼ pint orange juice
2 tablespoons lemon juice
2 level tablespoons sugar
1 level tablespoon cornflour
2 level tablespoons butter
salt

1. Peel and dice beetroot.

2. Heat orange rind with orange and lemon juice.

3. Mix sugar and cornflour, and stir into hot liquid. Cook, stirring constantly, until thickened. Add diced beetroot and butter. Season to taste with salt, and heat through.

Basic Boiled Broccoli

675-900 g/1½-2 lb fresh broccoli
salt
4 tablespoons olive oil or melted butter
lemon juice
freshly ground black pepper

1. Wash broccoli in cold water. Discard coarse leaves and tough lower parts of the stems. Soak prepared broccoli in salted water for 30 minutes. Drain.

2. Half fill a saucepan with water, add salt, to taste, and bring to the boil. Lower broccoli gently into boiling water, keeping flowerets out of the water. Cover saucepan and cook broccoli for about 15 minutes, or until barely tender.

3. Drain the broccoli, transfer to a heated serving dish, sprinkle with olive oil (or melted butter) and lemon juice. Season with salt and freshly ground black pepper and serve immediately.

Broccoli Towers

1 (283-g/10-oz) packet frozen broccoli
4-6 level tablespoons butter
150 ml/¼ pint chicken stock
salt
2 eggs
butter
6-8 level tablespoons grated cheese
freshly ground black pepper

1. Defrost broccoli. Slice thickly and place in a saucepan. Cover with cold water and cook over a high heat until water boils. Drain.

2. Simmer blanched broccoli in butter, chicken stock and salt, to taste, until broccoli has absorbed the liquid without burning and is quite tender.

3. Mash broccoli mixture and mix well with 2 eggs, 4 tablespoons softened butter, cheese, and salt and freshly ground black pepper, to taste. Press into 6 well-buttered dariole moulds. Place moulds in a roasting tin and add enough boiling water to come half-way up moulds. Heat in a moderate oven (180°C, 350°F, Gas Mark 4) for 20 minutes.

4. When ready to serve, turn broccoli moulds out on a heated serving dish. (If desired, surround with sautéed button mushrooms.)

Broccoli with Cheese Sauce and Slivered Almonds

Illustrated on page 87

450-675 g/1-1½ lb fresh or frozen broccoli
   spears
salt

CHEESE SAUCE
75 g/3 oz butter
2 level teaspoons Dijon mustard
75 g/3 oz flour
900 ml/1½ pints milk
225 g/8 oz grated Emmenthal cheese
salt and white pepper

GARNISH
50 g/2 oz almonds, blanched, slivered, fried
   in oil and seasoned

1. Cook the broccoli spears in boiling salted water until tender. Drain.

2. To make cheese sauce: melt the butter in a saucepan over a high heat, then stir in the mustard and flour. Add the milk gradually, stirring continuously. Lower the heat and cook, stirring, until the sauce comes to the boil. Boil the sauce for 2 minutes, then remove from the heat, stir in the grated cheese, and season to taste with salt and white pepper. Return to heat and let sauce simmer until thick and smooth.

3. Pour the cheese sauce over the broccoli spears. Sprinkle with slivered almonds. The dish may be lightly browned under the grill if desired.

55

56

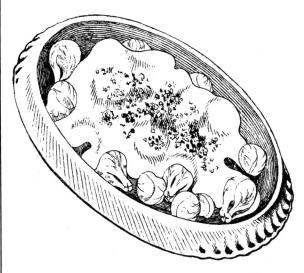

Brussels Sprouts au Gratin

450 g/1 lb small Brussels sprouts
salt
freshly ground black pepper
butter
600 ml/1 pint well-flavoured Cheese Sauce
(see Broccoli with Cheese Sauce and
Slivered Almonds, page 55)
4 walnuts, finely chopped
2 level tablespoons fresh breadcrumbs

1. To prepare Brussels sprouts: cut off stem
ends and remove any wilted or damaged outside
leaves. (If Brussels sprouts are older, remove
tough outside leaves entirely.) Soak sprouts in
cold water with a little salt or lemon juice for 15
minutes.

2. To cook Brussels sprouts: add to boiling
salted water and simmer uncovered for 5 minutes.
Cover pan and continue to cook for 7 (if very
young) to 15 minutes, or until just tender. Drain
well and season generously with salt and freshly
ground black pepper.

3. Place hot, seasoned sprouts in a well-buttered
ovenproof dish. Pour over well-flavoured cheese
sauce.

4. Melt 5 tablespoons butter in a small saucepan,
add finely chopped nuts and freshly grated breadcrumbs, simmer for a minute or two, then spoon
over cheese sauce. Bake in a moderately hot oven
(200°C, 400°F, Gas Mark 6) for 10 minutes.

Brussels Sprouts à la Polonaise
Illustrated on page 66

450 g/1 lb small Brussels sprouts
salt
freshly ground black pepper
4-6 tablespoons browned butter
grated rind and juice of 1 lemon
4 level tablespoons finely chopped parsley
whites of 2 hard-boiled eggs, finely chopped

1. To prepare Brussels sprouts: cut off stem
ends and remove any wilted or damaged outside
leaves. (If Brussels sprouts are older, remove tough
outside leaves entirely.) Soak sprouts in cold water
with a little salt or lemon juice for 15 minutes.

2. To cook Brussels sprouts: add sprouts to
boiling salted water and simmer uncovered for 5
minutes. Cover pan and continue to cook for 7
(if very young) to 15 minutes, or until just tender.
Drain well and season generously with salt and
freshly ground black pepper.

3. Place hot, seasoned sprouts in a heated serving
dish, pour browned butter over them, sprinkle to
taste with grated lemon rind, finely chopped
parsley and egg white, and lemon juice.

Brussels Sprouts with Buttered Breadcrumbs

450 g/1 lb small Brussels sprouts
salt
freshly ground black pepper
4-6 level tablespoons toasted breadcrumbs
½ clove garlic, finely chopped
4 level tablespoons butter
lemon juice

1. To prepare Brussels sprouts: cut off stem
ends and remove any wilted or damaged outside

leaves. (If Brussels sprouts are older, remove tough outside leaves entirely.) Soak sprouts in cold water with a little salt juice for 15 minutes.

2. To cook Brussels sprouts: add sprouts to boiling salted water and simmer uncovered for 5 minutes. Cover pan and continue to cook for 7 (if very young) to 15 minutes, or until just tender. Drain well and season generously with salt and freshly ground black pepper.

3. Combine hot, seasoned sprouts in a frying pan with toasted breadcrumbs and finely chopped garlic, and sauté in butter until breadcrumbs are golden. Sprinkle with lemon juice, to taste.

Brussels Sprouts in Beer Batter

450-675 g/1-1½ lb Brussels sprouts
salt or lemon juice
oil for deep-frying
1 egg
150 ml/¼ pint beer
100 g/4 oz flour
freshly ground black pepper
French Tomato Sauce (see page 90)

1. To prepare Brussels sprouts: cut off stem ends and remove any wilted or damaged outside leaves. (If Brussels sprouts are older, remove tough outside leaves entirely.) Soak sprouts in cold water with a little salt or lemon juice for 15 minutes.

2. To cook Brussels sprouts: add to boiling salted water and simmer, uncovered, for 7 (if very young) to 15 minutes, or until just tender. Drain.

3. To make Beer Batter: beat egg in a bowl, add beer and beat until smooth. Add flour and 1 level teaspoon salt, and freshly ground black pepper, to taste, and beat until smooth. Allow batter to rest for at least 30 minutes.

4. Heat oil to 190°C/375°F. Dip prepared Brussels sprouts into batter and deep-fry until golden. Drain and serve immediately with French Tomato Sauce.

Brussels Sprouts à la Provençale

57

450-675 g/1-1½ lb Brussels sprouts
salt
1 Spanish onion, finely chopped
2 small cloves garlic, finely chopped
3 tablespoons olive oil
½ level teaspoon chopped thyme
6 tomatoes, peeled and diced
2 level tablespoons finely chopped parsley
freshly ground black pepper
2 level tablespoons fresh breadcrumbs

1. Prepare and cook Brussels sprouts as in recipe above (Brussels Sprouts in Beer Batter), but for 5 minutes only.

2. Sauté onion and garlic in olive oil with chopped thyme until vegetables are transparent.

3. Add diced, peeled tomatoes and finely chopped parsley; season with salt and freshly ground black pepper.

4. Add cooked Brussels sprouts and breadcrumbs and simmer for a further 10 minutes, or until Brussels sprouts are tender.

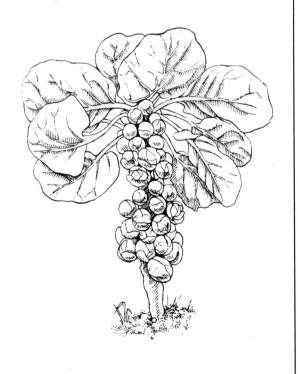

Red Cabbage *Serves 6 to 8*
Carrots à la Béchamel *Serves 4*
Carrots à l'Orientale *Serves 4*
Carrots aux Fines Herbes *Serves 4*

58

Red Cabbage

1 red cabbage (about 1 kg/2 lb)
2 level tablespoons bacon fat
3 tart red apples, cored and sliced
½ Spanish onion, finely chopped
1 clove garlic, finely chopped
2-4 tablespoons wine vinegar
1 level tablespoon flour
2 level tablespoons brown sugar
1 level teaspoon grated orange rind
salt and freshly ground black pepper
freshly grated nutmeg

1. Wash and shred cabbage, removing central core, ribs and outer leaves. Toss in bacon fat, in a covered saucepan, over a moderate heat for 5 minutes.

2. Add sliced apples and finely chopped onion and garlic, and bring to the boil with just enough water to cover. Cover, reduce heat, and simmer until tender but still crisp – about 15 minutes. Drain, reserving liquid.

3. Combine wine vinegar with flour and brown sugar, and stir in the reserved liquid. Cook, stirring, until thickened.

4. Stir into cabbage, add grated orange rind, and season to taste with salt, freshly ground black pepper and nutmeg.

Carrots à la Béchamel

450 g/1 lb carrots
4 level tablespoons butter
4 tablespoons chicken stock
sugar
salt and freshly ground black pepper
6 level tablespoons Béchamel Sauce (see page 89)

1. Wash carrots, slice thickly and place in a saucepan of cold water. Bring to the boil and drain.

2. Simmer carrots for 15 to 20 minutes in butter and chicken stock, with sugar, salt and freshly ground black pepper, to taste.

3. Just before serving, add Béchamel Sauce.

Carrots à l'Orientale

450 g/1 lb carrots
4 level tablespoons butter
4 tablespoons chicken stock
2 level tablespoons pre-soaked raisins
sugar
salt and freshly ground black pepper

1. Wash carrots, slice thickly and place in a saucepan of cold water. Bring to the boil and drain.

2. Simmer carrots for 15 to 20 minutes in butter and chicken stock, with pre-soaked raisins, sugar, salt and freshly ground black pepper, to taste.

Carrots aux Fines Herbes

450 g/1 lb carrots
4 level tablespoons butter
4 tablespoons chicken stock
sugar
salt and freshly ground black pepper
2 level tablespoons each chopped parsley and chervil

1. Wash carrots, slice thickly and place in a saucepan of cold water. Bring to the boil and drain.

2. Simmer carrots for 15 to 20 minutes in butter and chicken stock, with sugar, salt and freshly ground black pepper, to taste.

3. Just before serving, sprinkle with chopped parsley and chervil.

Pan-fried Carrots

8 small carrots
1 tablespoon olive oil
2 level tablespoons butter
salt and freshly ground black pepper
2 level tablespoons finely chopped parsley

1. Wash and scrape carrots, trim off ends and shred coarsely.

2. Sauté carrot strips in oil and butter, stirring constantly, until almost tender. Season generously with salt and freshly ground black pepper. Cover pan and cook over a low heat until tender (5 to 8 minutes in all).

3. Sprinkle with finely chopped parsley.

Carrot Ring Mould with Peas and Onions

Illustrated on page 66

1–1½ kg/2–3 lb new carrots
4–6 level tablespoons butter
150 ml/¼ pint chicken stock
1 level tablespoon sugar
salt
2 eggs
butter
6–8 level tablespoons grated cheese
freshly ground black pepper
cooked peas and button onions

1. Wash carrots, slice thickly and place in a saucepan. Cover with cold water and cook over a high heat until water boils. Drain.

2. Simmer blanched carrots in butter, chicken stock and sugar, with salt, to taste, until carrots have absorbed the liquid and are tender.

3. Mash carrot mixture and mix well with eggs, 4 tablespoons softened butter, cheese, and salt and freshly ground black pepper, to taste. Press into a well-buttered ring mould and heat through in a moderate oven (180°C, 350°F, Gas Mark 4) for 15 minutes.

4. Turn carrot ring out on a heated serving dish and fill centre with cooked peas and button onions. Surround with remaining peas and onions.

Carrot Towers

1 kg/2 lb new carrots
4–6 level tablespoons butter
150 ml/¼ pint chicken stock
1 level tablespoon sugar
salt
2 eggs
butter
6–8 level tablespoons grated cheese
freshly ground black pepper

GARNISH
button mushrooms (optional)

1. Wash carrots, slice thickly and place in a saucepan. Cover with cold water and cook over a high heat until water boils. Drain.

2. Simmer blanched carrots in butter, chicken stock and sugar, with salt, to taste, until carrots have absorbed the liquid without burning and are tender.

3. Mash carrot mixture and mix well with 2 eggs, 4 tablespoons softened butter, cheese, and salt and freshly ground black pepper, to taste. Press into 6 well-buttered dariole moulds.

4. Place moulds in a roasting tin and add enough boiling water to come half-way up moulds. Heat in a moderate oven (180°C, 350°F, Gas Mark 4) for 20 minutes.

5. When ready to serve, turn carrot moulds out on to heated serving dish and surround with sautéed button mushrooms (if desired).

60

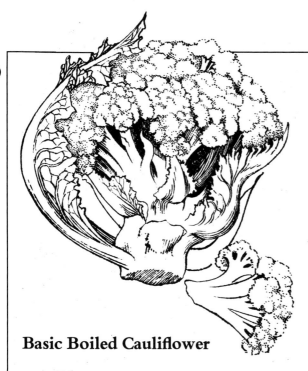

Basic Boiled Cauliflower

1 cauliflower
salt
melted butter
freshly ground black pepper

1. Trim off the base of a cauliflower, taking the remains of the outer leaves with it. Leave the fine, light green leaves intact. Using a potato peeler, hollow out the stem about 5 cm/2 inches deep.

2. Immerse cauliflower, head down, in a bowl of cold salted water.

3. Select a saucepan one size larger than the cauliflower. Pour in 5 cm/2 inches salted water and bring to the boil.

4. Lower cauliflower stem end down into boiling water. Bring back to the boil again before covering pan with a tight fitting lid. An average-sized cauliflower (about 700 g/1½ lb) will be cooked to perfection – tender but with a slight crispness still in evidence – in 15 minutes, but you may prefer it a little softer.

5. Remove cauliflower from pan and drain.

6. To serve: place it on a heated serving dish and pour over melted butter which you have generously seasoned with salt and freshly ground black pepper.

Cauliflower Amandine

1 cauliflower
salt
lemon juice
4 level tablespoons blanched slivered
    almonds
6 level tablespoons butter
freshly ground black pepper

1. To prepare cauliflower: trim stem and remove outer green leaves, wash and leave for 30 minutes in cold salted water to which you have added a little lemon juice.

2. To cook cauliflower: measure enough water to cover cauliflower into a deep saucepan. Add salt, to taste, and bring to the boil. Put cauliflower in the boiling water, bring to the boil again, then lower heat, cover saucepan and simmer gently for about 20 minutes, or until the cauliflower is just tender when pierced at the stem end with a fork. Do not overcook. Drain well.

3. Sauté blanched slivered almonds in butter, pour sauce over hot cauliflower, and season to taste with salt and freshly ground black pepper.

Cauliflower Sauté

1 cauliflower
salt
lemon juice
4 level tablespoons butter
2 level tablespoons finely chopped fresh
    herbs (chives, chervil, parsley)

1. To prepare cauliflower: trim stem and remove outer green leaves, cut into flowerets, wash and leave for 30 minutes in cold salted water to which you have added a little lemon juice.

2. To cook flowerets: measure enough water to cover cauliflowerets into a deep saucepan. Add salt, to taste, and bring to the boil. Put cauliflowerets in the boiling water, bring to the boil again, then lower heat, cover saucepan and simmer .gently for about 10 minutes, or until the cauliflowerets are almost tender when pierced at the stem end with a fork. Drain well.

3. Sauté cauliflowerets in butter and lemon juice until tender. Sprinkle with finely chopped fresh herbs and serve immediately.

Cauliflower à la Niçoise

1 cauliflower
salt
1 Spanish onion, finely chopped
1 clove garlic, finely chopped
2 tablespoons olive oil
2 level tablespoons butter
4 tomatoes, peeled and diced
2 level tablespoons finely chopped parsley
freshly ground black pepper
2 level tablespoons breadcrumbs

1. Prepare and cook cauliflower in salted boiling water as in Steps **1.** and **2.** of Cauliflower Sauté (see page 60).

2. Sauté finely chopped onion and garlic until transparent in olive oil and butter. Add diced, peeled tomatoes and finely chopped parsley. Season with salt and freshly ground black pepper. Add cooked cauliflowerets and breadcrumbs and simmer for a further 10 minutes, or until tender.

French Fried Cauliflower

1 cauliflower
1 egg
150 ml/¼ pint milk
100 g/4 oz flour
salt
oil for deep-frying
French Tomato Sauce (see page 90)

1. To make batter: beat egg in a bowl, add milk and beat. Add flour and 1 teaspoon salt and beat until smooth.

2. Prepare and cook cauliflower in salted boiling water as in Steps **1.** and **2.** of Cauliflower Sauté (see page 60).

3. Heat oil to 190°C/375°F.

4. Dip flowerets into batter. Deep fry until golden. Drain and serve immediately with French Tomato Sauce.

Pain de Chou-Fleur

1 whole cauliflower
salt
lemon juice
3 egg yolks, well beaten
softened butter
freshly ground black pepper
freshly grated nutmeg
300 ml/½ pint Hollandaise Sauce (see page 89)

1. To prepare cauliflower: trim stem and remove outer green leaves, wash and leave for 30 minutes in cold salted water to which you have added a little lemon juice.

2. To cook cauliflower: measure enough water to cover cauliflower into a deep saucepan. Add salt to taste, and bring to the boil. Put cauliflower in the boiling water, bring to the boil again, then lower heat, cover saucepan and simmer gently for about 20 minutes, or until the cauliflower is just tender when pierced at the stem end with a fork. Do not overcook. Drain well.

3. Force cauliflower through a fine sieve. Beat in well-beaten egg yolks and 4 tablespoons softened butter, and season to taste with salt, freshly ground black pepper and freshly grated nutmeg.

4. Pour mixture into a well-buttered soufflé dish or charlotte mould, and cook in a pan of hot water in a moderately hot oven (190°C, 375°F, Gas Mark 5) for 25 minutes.

5. Turn out on to a heated serving dish and mask with Hollandaise Sauce.

Basic Boiled Chicory

8 heads chicory
300 ml/½ pint salted water
4 level tablespoons butter
juice of ½ lemon
2 level tablespoons finely chopped parsley

1. Trim root ends of chicory and wash well in cold water. Drain.

2. Place chicory in a saucepan with boiling salted water, 2 tablespoons butter and lemon juice, and cook for 20 to 30 minutes, or until tender. Drain thoroughly, reserving juices.

3. **To serve chicory:** boil reserved pan juices until reduced a little, pour over cooked chicory, sprinkle with finely chopped parsley and top with remaining butter.

Chicory au Gratin

8 heads chicory
salt
juice of 1 lemon
4 thin slices cooked ham
butter
8 level tablespoons freshly grated Parmesan
  cheese
300-450 ml/½-¾ pint well-flavoured
  Béchamel Sauce (see page 89)
4 level tablespoons fresh breadcrumbs

1. Trim root ends of chicory and wash well in cold water. Drain. Place chicory in a saucepan of boiling salted water with lemon juice, and simmer for 30 minutes. Drain well. Press in a clean cloth to remove excess moisture.

2. Roll each head in half a slice of ham and arrange in a well-buttered shallow ovenproof casserole.

3. Mix freshly grated Parmesan into Béchamel Sauce and pour over chicory. Sprinkle with fresh breadcrumbs and 2 tablespoons melted butter, and cook in a moderately hot oven (200°C, 400°F, Gas Mark 6) for 10 to 15 minutes, until golden.

Chicory Soufflé

225 g/8 oz braised chicory
butter
freshly grated Parmesan cheese
2 tablespoons lemon juice
5 egg yolks
2 level tablespoons grated onion
salt and freshly ground black pepper
6 egg whites

1. Pass braised chicory through a sieve and dry it out over a low heat in 1 tablespoon butter, stirring all the time with a wooden spoon to keep it from sticking. Stir in 50 g/2 oz freshly grated Parmesan and 2 tablespoons lemon juice.

2. Remove from the heat and stir in egg yolks one at a time. Season rather strongly with grated onion, salt and freshly ground black pepper. Beat egg whites until stiff but not dry and fold into soufflé mixture.

3. Butter a soufflé dish, dust with a little grated Parmesan cheese and fill with the mixture. Place in a preheated moderate oven (180°C, 350°F, Gas Mark 4) and bake for 25 to 35 minutes.

Chicory à la Béchamel

8 heads chicory
300 ml/½ pint salted water
4 level tablespoons butter
juice of ½ lemon
300-450 ml/½-¾ pint well-flavoured
  Béchamel Sauce (see page 89)

1. Trim root ends of chicory and wash well in cold water. Drain.

2. Place chicory in a saucepan with boiling salted water, butter and lemon juice, and cook for 20 to 30 minutes, or until tender. Drain thoroughly, reserving juices.

3. Place chicory in a shallow ovenproof baking dish. Add drained pan juices to hot Béchamel Sauce. Pour sauce over chicory and serve immediately.

Chinese Mushrooms *Serves 4*
Chinese Peas with Ham *Serves 4*
Chinese Braised Vegetables *Serves 4*
Chinese Spinach *Serves 4*

63

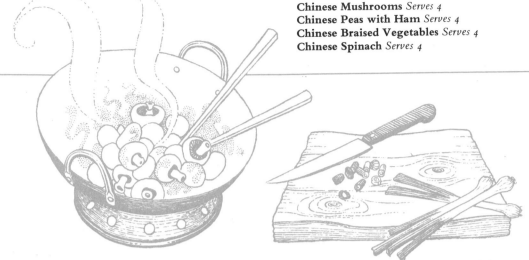

Chinese Mushrooms

2 tablespoons peanut oil or lard
225 g/8 oz mushrooms
½ tablespoon salt
150 ml/¼ pint water
1 level teaspoon cornflour

1. Heat oil or lard in a *wok* or frying pan. Add mushrooms and salt and stir over medium heat for 1 minute. Add water, cover pan and simmer for 3 minutes.

2. Remove cover, add cornflour and simmer until thickened. Serve immediately.

Chinese Peas with Ham

450 g/1 lb frozen peas, defrosted
2 level tablespoons finely chopped spring
   onions
4 level tablespoons butter
1 slice of cooked ham, 5 mm/¼ inch thick
soy sauce or lemon juice
salt and freshly ground black pepper

1. Place peas in a shallow *gratin* dish or bowl with finely chopped spring onions and 2 level tablespoons butter, and steam over boiling water in a tightly closed saucepan or double steamer for 15 minutes, or until tender.

2. Cut cooked ham into thin strips and sauté gently in remaining butter.

3. Combine with steamed peas and flavour to taste with soy sauce (or lemon juice), salt and freshly ground black pepper.

Chinese Braised Vegetables
Illustrated on page 86

1 head celery
225 g/8 oz button mushrooms
3 tablespoons peanut oil
½ level teaspoon salt
¼ level teaspoon monosodium glutamate
   (optional)
1–2 tablespoons soy sauce
1 level teaspoon sugar

1. Cut the celery sticks diagonally into 2.5-cm/ 1-inch lengths. Wash the mushrooms and trim their stems.

2. Heat the oil in a thick-bottomed frying pan and sauté the celery and mushrooms, stirring frequently. Add the remaining ingredients to the pan and mix well. Continue cooking until the celery is just tender. Serve hot, with the pan juices poured over the top.

Chinese Spinach
Illustrated on page 86

1 kg/2 lb fresh spinach leaves
3 tablespoons peanut oil or lard
1 level teaspoon salt
1 tablespoon soy sauce, sake or dry sherry

1. Wash spinach leaves in several changes of water. Drain and dry thoroughly.

2. Heat oil or lard in a *wok* or frying pan. Add spinach and salt and cook over a medium heat for 3 minutes, stirring constantly. Add soy sauce, *sake* or dry sherry, to taste. Serve immediately.

64

Chinese Courgettes

450 g/1 lb courgettes
2 tablespoons peanut oil or lard
1 level teaspoon salt
150 ml/¼ pint water
1 tablespoon soy sauce
1 tablespoon sake or dry sherry

1. Wash courgettes, cut off ends and slice thinly.

2. Heat oil or lard in a *wok* or frying pan; add courgettes and salt and cook over medium heat for 3 minutes, stirring continuously. Add water, stir in and heat through. Add soy sauce and *sake* or dry sherry, to taste. Serve immediately.

Courgettes with Walnuts

8 walnuts
8 small courgettes
1 tablespoon olive oil
2 level tablespoons butter
salt and freshly ground black pepper

1. Shell walnuts and chop coarsely.

2. Cut unpeeled courgettes in 3-mm/⅛-inch slices. Sauté in oil and butter, stirring constantly, until courgettes are almost tender.

3. Add chopped walnuts and salt and freshly ground black pepper, to taste, and continue to cook over a low heat until done.

New Courgettes Hollandaise

450 g/1 lb courgettes
2 tablespoons peanut oil or lard
salt and freshly ground black pepper
150 ml/¼ pint water
1 tablespoon soy sauce
1 tablespoon dry sherry
300 ml/½ pint Hollandaise Sauce (see page 89)

1. Wash courgettes, cut off ends and slice very thinly.

2. Heat oil or lard in a large, thick-bottomed frying pan; add thinly sliced courgettes, and salt and freshly ground black pepper, to taste, and cook over medium heat for 3 minutes, stirring continuously. Add water and soy sauce and dry sherry, and cook for a few minutes more. Drain.

3. Transfer cooked courgettes to 4 individual flameproof *gratin* dishes. Top with Hollandaise Sauce and place under a preheated grill for a few seconds, watching carefully, until sauce begins to turn golden brown. Serve immediately.

Glazed Sliced Courgettes

12 courgettes
4 level tablespoons butter
4 level tablespoons chicken stock
salt and freshly ground black pepper
sugar
finely chopped parsley

Cut unpeeled courgettes into thin slices. Combine in a shallow saucepan with butter, chicken stock, salt and freshly ground black pepper and sugar, to taste. Simmer gently, covered, until liquid has almost disappeared and courgettes are glazed and tender. Sprinkle with finely chopped parsley and serve immediately.

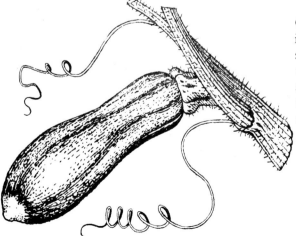

Still Life of Winter Vegetables

Carrot Ring Mould with Peas and Onions
(see page 59)
Brussels Sprouts à la Polonaise (see page 56)

Leeks Béchamel (see page 70)

Oven-baked Potatoes with Soured Cream and Chive Dressing (see page 80)

Courgettes in Red Wine *Serves 4*
Stuffed Courgettes à la Provençale *Serves 4*
Courgettes Soufflées *Serves 4*
Mrs Glasse's Stew'd Cucumbers

Courgettes in Red Wine

12 courgettes
100 g/4 oz finely chopped Spanish onion
4 tablespoons olive oil
2 level tablespoons butter
150 ml/¼ pint red wine
salt and freshly ground black pepper
lemon juice and olive oil
finely chopped parsley

1. Cut courgettes into slices 1 cm/½ inch thick and sauté with finely chopped onion in olive oil and butter for 5 minutes, stirring frequently.

2. Add wine, and season to taste with salt and freshly ground black pepper. Simmer for 5 minutes.

3. Just before serving, sprinkle with a little lemon juice, olive oil and finely chopped parsley.

Stuffed Courgettes à la Provençale

12 courgettes (for cases)
salt
olive oil
butter

PROVENÇAL STUFFING
175 g/6 oz minced veal
25 g/1 oz fat salt pork, diced
1 onion, finely chopped
olive oil
1 clove garlic, crushed
minced fresh tarragon
minced fresh parsley
1 egg, beaten
1 tablespoon grated Parmesan cheese
4 tablespoons boiled rice
courgette pulp
salt and freshly ground black pepper

1. Simmer courgettes whole in salted water for about 5 minutes. Cut tops off courgettes, scoop out interiors and keep pulp for stuffing.

2. **To make stuffing:** sauté meats and onion in olive oil. Mix remaining ingredients in a bowl and add them to the meat and onion mixture, adding salt and freshly ground black pepper, to taste. Sauté for a few minutes, stirring continuously, and then stuff courgettes with the mixture.

3. Place stuffed courgettes in an ovenproof baking dish to which you have added a little olive oil. Place a knob of butter on each courgette and bake in a moderate oven (190°C, 375°F, Gas Mark 5) for 30 minutes.

Courgettes Soufflées

6 courgettes
2–4 level tablespoons butter
salt and freshly ground black pepper
150 ml/¼ pint Béchamel Sauce (see page 89)
2 egg yolks
freshly grated Parmesan cheese
2 egg whites

1. Wash the courgettes and cut them in two lengthwise. Scoop out the flesh, being careful not to pierce the skin. Cook the pulp in butter until it becomes a thick purée. Season generously with salt and freshly ground black pepper.

2. Make a Béchamel Sauce. Remove the sauce from the heat and beat in the egg yolks, one by one. Add the cooked courgette pulp and freshly grated Parmesan. Check seasoning. Beat the egg whites until stiff and fold gently into the mixture.

3. Place the courgette shells in a buttered baking dish. Fill with the soufflé mixture and bake for 25 minutes in a moderate oven (160°C, 325°F, Gas Mark 3). Serve immediately.

Mrs. Glasse's Stew'd Cucumbers

'Pare twelve Cucumbers, and slice them as thick as a Crown piece, and put them to drain, and then lay them in a coarse Cloth till they are dry, flour them and fry them Brown in Butter; pour out the Fat, then put to them some Gravy, a little Claret, some Pepper, Cloves, and Mace, and let them stew a little; then roll a Bit of Butter in Flour, and toss them up seasoned with Salt.'

70

Braised Fennel

4 fennel roots
juice of ½ lemon
2 tablespoons olive oil or butter
150 ml/¼ pint chicken stock
salt and freshly ground black pepper
2 level teaspoons butter
2 level teaspoons flour
finely chopped parsley

1. Wash and trim fennel roots, and cut in half lengthwise.

2. Put fennel roots in an ovenproof dish with lemon juice, olive oil or butter, and stock. Season to taste with salt and freshly ground black pepper, then cover pan and cook slowly until tender – 30 to 40 minutes.

3. Five minutes before you remove vegetables from heat, stir in butter and flour, mixed to a smooth paste.

4. Just before serving, sprinkle with finely chopped parsley.

Basic Boiled Leeks

12 small or 8 large leeks
salted water
2–3 level tablespoons finely chopped parsley
melted butter

1. Trim roots and cut off the tops of leeks, leaving 2.5 cm/1 inch to 7.5 cm/3 inches of the green portion. Halve the leeks, leaving the halves attached at the root end. Wash thoroughly.

2. Simmer leeks in boiling salted water for 20 minutes, or until tender. Drain thoroughly. Sprinkle with finely chopped parsley and serve with melted butter.

Leeks in Butter

12 small or 8 large leeks
100 g/4 oz butter
salt and freshly ground black pepper

1. Trim roots and cut off the tops of leeks, leaving 2.5 cm/1 inch to 7.5 cm/3 inches of the green portion. Halve the leeks, leaving the halves attached at the root end. Wash thoroughly.

2. Simmer leeks in boiling water for 5 minutes. Drain thoroughly.

3. Place leeks in a shallow ovenproof baking dish; add butter, and salt and freshly ground black pepper, to taste, and cook in a moderately hot oven (190°C, 375°F, Gas Mark 5) for 35 to 40 minutes, or until tender.

Leeks Béchamel
Illustrated on page 67

12 small or 8 large leeks
100 g/4 oz butter
salt and freshly ground black pepper
300–450 ml/½–¾ pint well-flavoured
   Béchamel Sauce (see page 89)

1. Trim roots and cut off the tops of leeks, leaving 2.5 cm/1 inch to 7.5 cm/3 inches of the green portion. Halve the leeks, leaving the halves attached at the root end. Wash thoroughly.

2. Simmer leeks in boiling water for 5 minutes. Drain thoroughly.

3. Place leeks in a shallow ovenproof baking dish; add butter, and salt and freshly ground black pepper, to taste, and cook in a moderately hot oven (190°C, 375°F, Gas Mark 5) for 35 to 40 minutes, or until tender.

4. Drain pan juices and add to well-flavoured Béchamel Sauce. Pour over leeks and serve immediately.

2. Drain lentils and cook with onion in salted water until tender. The length of time for cooking lentils depends on their type and their age. In any case, after 30 minutes look at them from time to time to see if they are cooked. When ready, drain.

3. Heat olive oil in a saucepan, add finely chopped garlic and lentils, and continue to cook, shaking pan from time to time, until lentils are heated through.

4. Pound anchovy fillets and butter to a smooth paste, and add to lentils, stirring in well. Season to taste with salt and freshly ground black pepper. Place in serving dish and serve very hot.

Lentils Provençale

450 g/1 lb lentils
1 Spanish onion
salt
4-6 tablespoons olive oil
1 clove garlic, finely chopped
1 (56-g/2-oz) can anchovy fillets
100 g/4 oz butter
freshly ground black pepper

1. Place lentils in a large saucepan. Fill pan with water and bring gently to the boil. Remove saucepan from heat and let lentils soak in hot water for 1 hour.

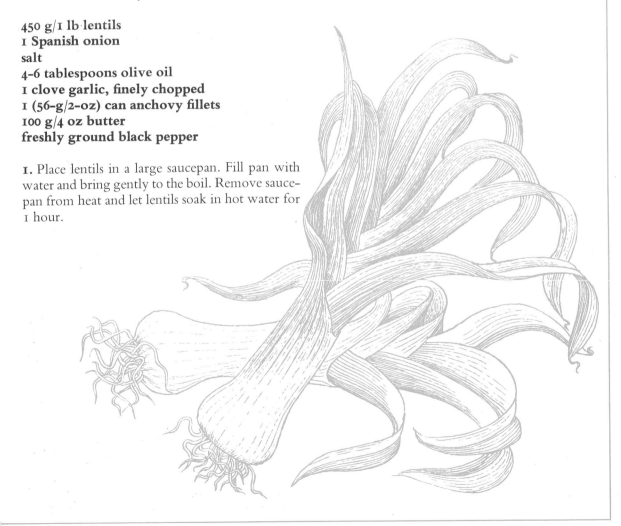

72

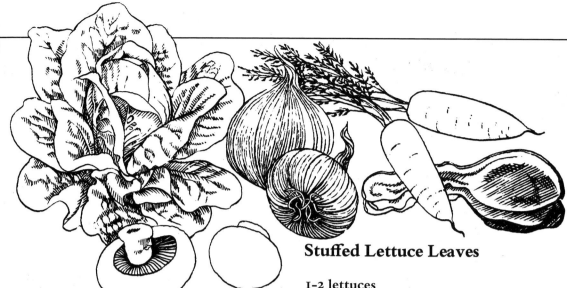

Braised Lettuce

4-6 small Cos lettuces
butter
1 rasher bacon, diced
½ Spanish onion, thinly sliced
2 small carrots, thinly sliced
150 ml/¼ pint chicken stock
salt and freshly ground black pepper
2 level teaspoons flour
finely chopped parsley

1. Clean lettuces, leaving them whole. Pare the base of each lettuce to a point. Drop lettuces into a large saucepan filled with boiling water, and boil for 5 minutes.

2. Pour off water and plunge lettuces into a bowl of cold water for a few minutes. Drain lettuces and press out excess moisture.

3. Butter an ovenproof dish. Place lettuces, diced bacon, and thinly sliced onion and carrots in dish, and add chicken stock. Season to taste with salt and freshly ground black pepper, then cover and cook slowly until tender – about 45 minutes.

4. About 5 minutes before you remove vegetables from heat, stir in 2 teaspoons butter which you have mixed to a smooth paste with 2 level teaspoons flour.

5. Just before serving, sprinkle with parsley.

Stuffed Lettuce Leaves

1-2 lettuces
2 level tablespoons butter
100 g/4 oz uncooked rice
600 ml/1 pint hot beef stock
½ Spanish onion, finely chopped
50 g/2 oz chopped mushrooms
2 tablespoons olive oil
100 g/4 oz ham, finely chopped
salt and freshly ground black pepper
2 level tablespoons tomato purée
2 level tablespoons finely chopped parsley

1. Separate lettuce leaves and wash well. Drain.

2. Melt butter in a thick-bottomed frying pan. Add rice, and sauté until golden. Cover with 300 ml/½ pint hot beef stock, adding a little water if necessary, and cook, stirring constantly, until the mixture comes to the boil. Reduce heat, cover pan, and cook slowly for about 15 minutes, adding a little more beef stock if necessary.

3. Sauté chopped onion and mushrooms in oil, and add to rice mixture. Mix in the finely chopped ham and season well.

4. Place equal quantities of the mixture on each lettuce leaf, and roll up, tucking ends in, to form neat 'packages'. Arrange them in a flat ovenproof dish.

5. Blend tomato purée with remaining 300 ml/½ pint hot beef stock, pour over stuffed lettuce leaves and bake in a moderately hot oven (190°C, 375°F, Gas Mark 5) for 30 minutes, or until done, basting frequently. Sprinkle with finely chopped parsley.

Mushrooms en Brochette

Illustrated on page 88

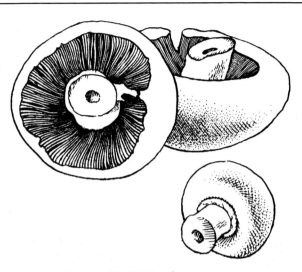

36 button mushrooms (about 1 kg/2 lb)
6 tablespoons melted butter
2 tablespoons olive oil
lemon juice
salt and freshly ground black pepper
finely chopped garlic
crushed rosemary

1. Clean mushrooms, remove stems (saving them for another use) and place 6 mushroom caps on each of 6 metal skewers.

2. Combine melted butter and olive oil, and flavour to taste with lemon juice, salt, freshly ground black pepper, garlic and rosemary.

3. Brush mushrooms with this mixture. Grill over charcoal or under the grill, turning mushrooms to brown them on all sides, and basting from time to time with sauce. Serve with grilled beef steak or lamb chops.

Sautéed Mushrooms Hong Kong

450 g/1 lb button mushrooms
100 g/4 oz cooked chicken breast
4 tablespoons peanut oil or lard
2 tablespoons sake, or dry white wine or dry sherry
1 tablespoon light soy sauce
½ level teaspoon sugar
½ level teaspoon cornflour

1. Wipe mushrooms and trim stems. Cut chicken into short thin matchsticks. Heat oil or lard in a Chinese *wok* or frying pan, add chicken and sauté until golden.

2. Add mushrooms and stir over medium heat for 1 minute. Add *sake* (or dry white wine or dry sherry) and soy sauce and sugar; cover pan and simmer for 3 minutes.

3. Remove cover. Add cornflour, mixed with a tablespoon or two of water, and simmer until sauce is slightly thickened. Serve immediately.

Spinach Stuffed Mushrooms

16–24 open button mushrooms, according to size
4 shallots, finely chopped
1 clove garlic, finely chopped
225 g/8 oz cooked spinach, chopped
¼ level teaspoon dried thyme
2 bay leaves, crumbled
1 egg, beaten
olive oil
salt and freshly ground black pepper
breadcrumbs
2 tablespoons finely chopped parsley
4 tablespoons dry white wine

1. Wipe mushrooms and trim stem ends. Remove stems from caps and chop finely. Combine chopped stems, shallots and garlic with chopped spinach, herbs and beaten egg. Moisten with a little olive oil. Season with salt and freshly ground black pepper, to taste, and sauté mixture in a little olive oil.

2. Fill mushroom caps with spinach mixture. Sprinkle lightly with breadcrumbs and finely chopped parsley.

3. Pour 4 tablespoons olive oil and dry white wine into a flameproof *gratin* dish and heat through on top of the cooker. Arrange stuffed mushroom caps in the dish and cook in a preheated moderate oven (190°C, 375°F, Gas Mark 5) for 15 to 20 minutes.

73

74

and bake in a moderately hot oven (190°C, 375°F, Gas Mark 5) for 15 to 20 minutes.

Onions and Carrots

350 g/12 oz small white onions
350 g/12 oz small carrots
4 level tablespoons butter
4 tablespoons chicken stock
salt
1 level tablespoon sugar

1. Peel onions.

2. Scrape carrots and slice them thickly.

3. Place vegetables in a saucepan, cover with cold water and cook over a high heat until water boils. Remove from heat and drain.

4. Replace vegetables in the saucepan, add butter and chicken stock, season to taste with salt and sugar, and simmer over a low heat until vegetables have absorbed all the liquid without burning, and have taken on a little colour.

Creamed Onions with Cloves

48 small white onions
salt
4 level tablespoons butter
8 whole cloves
1 level teaspoon sugar
freshly ground black pepper
1 level tablespoon flour
300 ml/½ pint cream
freshly grated Parmesan cheese

1. Peel onions and cook in boiling salted water, uncovered, until almost tender. Drain, and rinse in cold water.

2. Melt 3 level tablespoons butter in a large frying pan or casserole.

3. Stick 8 onions with cloves. Add all the onions to the melted butter, sprinkle with sugar and cook over a low heat, shaking pan frequently, until onions are golden brown on all sides.

4. Transfer onions and pan juices to a shallow baking dish. Season to taste with salt and freshly ground black pepper.

5. Melt remaining butter in a small saucepan, add flour and stir until smooth. Add cream and cook, stirring constantly, until sauce is thick. Pour sauce over onions, sprinkle with freshly grated Parmesan

Onion and Potato Gratinée

1 kg/2 lb Spanish onions, peeled
1 kg/2 lb large potatoes
300 ml/½ pint milk
6 level tablespoons freshly grated Parmesan
  cheese
4 eggs, well beaten
freshly grated nutmeg
salt and freshly ground black pepper
4 level tablespoons fresh breadcrumbs
2 tablespoons melted butter

1. Put peeled whole onions in a large saucepan, cover with cold water and bring slowly to the boil. Drain. Cover with fresh hot water and cook until tender. Drain.

2. Peel potatoes and boil them.

3. Put onions and potatoes through a *mouli-légumes*, or 'rice' them. Add milk, grated cheese and well-beaten eggs. Beat mixture until soft and creamy, season to taste with freshly grated nutmeg, salt and freshly ground black pepper. Place in an ovenproof dish and sprinkle with breadcrumbs and melted butter. Bake in a moderate oven (160°C, 325°F, Gas Mark 3) for 40 to 45 minutes.

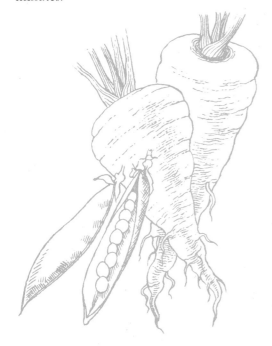

Cider-glazed Parsnips

12-18 small parsnips
salt
3 level tablespoons brown sugar
6-8 tablespoons cider
3 level tablespoons butter
freshly ground black pepper

1. Preheat oven to moderately hot (200°C, 400°F, Gas Mark 6).

2. Scrape parsnips and cut into quarters lengthwise. Cook in boiling water which has been salted until just tender. Drain.

3. Put parsnips in a shallow baking dish, sprinkle with sugar and cider, dot with butter, season with salt and freshly ground black pepper to taste and bake for 20 minutes, basting parsnips occasionally with glaze.

Garden Peas in Cream

75

675 g/1½ lb fresh peas in the pod
3 level tablespoons butter
150 ml/¼ pint water
¼ chicken stock cube
6 lettuce leaves, coarsely shredded
2 level tablespoons chopped onion
2 level tablespoons chopped parsley
1 level teaspoon sugar
salt and freshly ground black pepper
4-6 level tablespoons double cream

1. Shell peas.

2. Heat butter, water and stock cube to boiling point. Add peas, lettuce, chopped onion, parsley, and sugar, salt and freshly ground black pepper, to taste.

3. Cover pan and simmer over a low heat until peas are tender – 8 to 15 minutes. Remove pan from heat, stir in double cream and serve.

Hasty Peas and Onions

350 g/12 oz frozen peas
350 g/12 oz small button onions
6 level tablespoons butter
6 tablespoons chicken stock
2 level tablespoons sugar
salt and freshly ground black pepper

1. Place peas in a small saucepan, cover with cold water and cook over a high flame until the water boils. Remove from the heat and drain.

2. Place button onions in a saucepan, cover with cold water and bring to the boil. Lower heat and simmer for 10 minutes. Remove from the heat and drain.

3. Combine peas and onions in a large saucepan, add butter and chicken stock. Season with sugar and salt and freshly ground black pepper, to taste.

4. Simmer over a low flame until the vegetables have absorbed the liquid and are tender.

76

Roman Peas

**4 level tablespoons finely chopped
    Parma ham**
½ Spanish onion, finely chopped
butter
450 g/1 lb shelled peas, fresh or frozen
150 ml/¼ pint well-flavoured beef stock
sugar
salt and freshly ground black pepper
2 level tablespoons finely chopped parsley

1. Sauté finely chopped ham and onion in 4 table-spoons butter until onion begins to take on colour.

2. Add peas and beef stock, and season to taste with sugar, salt and freshly ground black pepper. Simmer peas, covered, for 10 to 15 minutes.

3. Just before serving, top with finely chopped parsley and a knob of butter.

Purée Saint-Germain

1 kg/2 lb frozen peas
1 lettuce heart, shredded
**12 tiny spring onions, or ½ Spanish onion,
    sliced**
3 sprigs parsley
100 g/4 oz butter
4 tablespoons chicken stock or water
sugar
salt
2 boiled potatoes, puréed (optional)

1. Put peas in a saucepan with the shredded heart of a lettuce, spring onions, parsley, half the butter, chicken stock or water, and sugar and salt, to taste. Bring to the boil and cook slowly until peas are tender.

2. When cooked, remove parsley and drain, reserving juices.

3. Blend to a fine purée in an electric blender (or press through a fine sieve) and reheat in the top of a double saucepan, adding a little of the strained juices and the remaining butter. If purée is too thin, add puréed potatoes to lend body.

Buttered Peas Elysées

450 g/1 lb frozen peas
4 level tablespoons butter
4 tablespoons chicken stock
salt and freshly ground black pepper
1 level tablespoon sugar
4 lettuce leaves, cut into thin strips
1 egg yolk
4 level tablespoons double cream

1. Place peas in a small saucepan, add enough cold water to just cover peas and cook over a high heat until the water boils. Remove from the heat and drain.

2. Replace peas in the saucepan, add butter and chicken stock, season to taste with salt and freshly ground black pepper and sugar. Cover with lettuce strips and simmer over a low heat until the peas have absorbed the liquid and are tender.

3. Combine egg yolk and double cream and stir into hot peas and lettuce. Serve immediately.

Note: Frozen peas cooked in this manner may also be puréed to serve as a vegetable or fold into a soufflé; or thinned with cream and well-flavoured chicken stock, to serve as a delicious soup.

Peas au Gratin

100 g/4 oz diced cooked ham
½ Spanish onion, finely chopped
butter
450 g/1 lb cooked peas, fresh or frozen
300 ml/½ pint cream, warmed
salt and freshly ground black pepper
2-4 level tablespoons freshly grated
    Parmesan cheese
2-4 level tablespoons freshly grated
    Gruyère cheese

1. Sauté diced ham and finely chopped onion in 2 tablespoons butter until onion begins to take on colour.

2. Combine ham and onion with cooked peas and warmed cream, and season to taste with salt and freshly ground black pepper. Pour mixture into a well-buttered casserole, sprinkle with freshly grated cheeses, dot with butter and cook under grill until top is golden.

Green Pea Pudding

450 g/1 lb split peas
1 (226-g/8-oz) packet frozen peas
50 g/2 oz butter
salt and freshly ground black pepper
3 eggs
flour

1. Soak split peas in water overnight. Drain. Defrost frozen peas.

2. Combine split peas and frozen peas and tie them in a thick pudding cloth, allowing enough room to swell. Cover them with cold water, bring to the boil and cook gently for 2 hours.

3. Lift pudding into a colander; drain well then untie cloth.

4. Rub peas through a sieve. Add butter and salt and freshly ground black pepper and mix well. Beat eggs until foamy and blend into the pudding gradually. Tie the mixture tightly in a well-floured pudding cloth and boil it again for 1 hour.

Stuffed Green Peppers

Illustrated on page 85

4-6 green peppers
olive oil
butter
salt and freshly ground black pepper
1 Spanish onion, finely chopped
450 g/1 lb pork sausagemeat
freshly grated nutmeg
2 level tablespoons grated Parmesan cheese
2 level tablespoons chopped chives
2 level tablespoons chopped parsley
300 ml/½ pint chicken stock (made with
    a cube)
strips of canned pimento

1. Remove the tops of the peppers. Remove pith and seeds. Place peppers in boiling water, to cover. Add 2 tablespoons olive oil and leave for 5 minutes. Drain well and dry.

2. Place a small piece of butter in the bottom of each pepper and season well. Sauté finely chopped onion in 4 tablespoons olive oil until onion is soft. Add crumbled sausagemeat and continue to cook, stirring constantly, until meat just begins to brown. Add salt, freshly ground black pepper, freshly grated nutmeg, grated Parmesan cheese, chopped chives and parsley and mix well.

3. Stuff peppers with this mixture and place in a flat, ovenproof dish. Pour chicken stock over peppers and bake in a preheated moderately hot oven (190°C, 375°F, Gas Mark 5) for 30 to 40 minutes, or until done, basting frequently. Just before serving, garnish each pepper with narrow strips of canned pimento.

78

Basic Boiled Potatoes

675–900 g/1½–2 lb new potatoes
coarse salt
butter
freshly ground black pepper

1. Wash potatoes and either scrape them or, if they peel easily, simply rub off a neat band of skin round the middle of each potato with your finger.

2. Put the potatoes in a pan. Cover with cold water, add a small handful of coarse salt and bring to the boil.

3. Simmer potatoes until they feel soft when pierced with a fork. Small ones will take about 18 minutes.

4. Drain well and serve with plenty of butter and coarse salt and freshly ground black pepper, to taste.

Mrs. Beeton's German Potatoes

75 g/3 oz butter
2 level tablespoons flour
300 ml/½ pint broth
2 tablespoons vinegar
8–10 medium-sized potatoes
1 bay leaf (optional)

'Put the butter and flour into a stew pan; stir over the fire until the butter is of a nice brown colour, and add the broth and vinegar; peel and cut the potatoes into long thin slices, lay them in the gravy, and let them simmer gently until tender, which will be from 10 to 15 minutes, and serve very hot. A laurel-leaf (bay leaf) simmered with the potatoes is an improvement.'

Scalloped Potatoes with Cheese

4 large baking potatoes
butter
225 g/8 oz Cheddar cheese, grated
1 Spanish onion, finely chopped
4 level tablespoons finely chopped parsley
salt and freshly ground black pepper
½ level teaspoon paprika
450 ml/¾ pint milk
150 ml/¼ pint double cream

1. Peel potatoes and slice them thinly. Soak sliced potatoes in cold water for 10 minutes. Drain and dry carefully.

2. Butter a shallow baking dish generously and cover bottom of dish with a layer of potatoes. Season to taste with grated cheese (reserving 4 tablespoons for later use), onion, parsley, salt, freshly ground black pepper and paprika. Cover with another layer of potatoes and season as above. Cover with remaining potatoes, pour in milk and cream to cover, and bake in a hot oven (230°C, 450°F, Gas Mark 8) for 10 minutes.

3. Reduce oven heat to (180°C, 350°F, Gas Mark 4), sprinkle with remaining cheese and bake until the potatoes are tender – about 2 hours.

Buttered New Potatoes with Chicken or Goose Fat

675-900 g/1½-2 lb tiny new potatoes
salt
4 level tablespoons chicken or goose fat
4 level tablespoons butter
4 level tablespoons finely chopped parsley
freshly ground black pepper

1. Scrub the skin from potatoes, place them in a large casserole, add enough salted water to just cover and parboil them for 3 minutes. Drain.

2. Heat chicken or goose fat in a large frying pan, add potatoes and cook, shaking pan frequently, until potatoes are tender and golden brown on all sides.

3. Remove potatoes from pan with a slotted spoon and pour off fat from the pan. Return potatoes to the pan, add butter and continue to cook for a few minutes, rolling potatoes in the butter as it melts.

4. Just before serving, sprinkle with finely chopped parsley and season with salt and freshly ground black pepper, to taste.

Gratin Dauphinois

450 g/1 lb new potatoes
2 level tablespoons butter
1 egg
150 ml/¼ pint double cream
8 level tablespoons freshly grated Gruyère cheese
4 level tablespoons freshly grated Parmesan cheese
salt and freshly ground black pepper

1. Peel or scrape potatoes and slice them very thinly (about 1 mm/1/16 inch thick). Rinse thoroughly and leave to soak in a bowl of cold water for 15 minutes. Select a shallow ovenproof dish about 23 cm/9 inches by 13 cm/5 inches. Grease with 2 level teaspoons of the butter.

2. Preheat oven to cool (150°C, 300°F, Gas Mark 2).

3. Drain potato slices and dry them thoroughly with a cloth or absorbent paper.

4. Whisk egg and cream together until well blended.

5. Arrange a quarter of the potato slices in the dish in overlapping rows; pour over 2 level tablespoons egg and cream mixture; sprinkle with 2 level tablespoons Gruyère and 1 level tablespoon Parmesan; dot with 1 level teaspoon butter; and finally, season to taste with salt and freshly ground black pepper.

6. Repeat layers exactly as above, making four in all, and ending with grated cheese and butter.

7. Bake *gratin* for 1 hour 20 minutes, or until potatoes feel tender when pierced with a sharp skewer and are golden and bubbling on top.

8. Allow to 'settle' for a few minutes before serving.

Note: If top browns too quickly, cover with a sheet of foil. If you use old potatoes, the cooking time will be slightly shorter.

Pommes de Terre Soufflées

900 ml/1½ pints peanut oil
675 g/1½ lb new potatoes, peeled, dried and thinly sliced
salt
deep fryer, with frying basket

1. Heat the oil. Place sliced potatoes in a frying basket and plunge them into the hot oil. They should begin to colour in a few minutes. Remove basket from oil and allow potatoes to cool.

2. When ready to serve: heat the oil again, this time a little hotter than before (this is the magic trick that makes the twice-fried potatoes swell up into feather-light 'balloons', but you'll have to practise to make perfect), and plunge the basket of sliced potatoes into it again. Continue to cook until potatoes are puffed and golden. Drain, season with salt, and serve immediately.

Pommes de Terre Duchesse *Serves 4 to 6*
Pommes de Terre en Daube *Serves 4 to 6*
Oven-baked Potatoes with Soured Cream and Chive
Dressing *Serves 4*

80

Pommes de Terre Duchesse

1 kg/2 lb potatoes
salt
butter
2 eggs
2 egg yolks
freshly ground black pepper
freshly ground nutmeg

1. Peel potatoes and slice them thickly. Cook them, covered, in simmering salted water until soft but not mushy. Drain well. Return potatoes to pan and remove all moisture by shaking pan over heat until they are dry.

2. Rub potatoes through a fine sieve, add 2 to 4 tablespoons butter, beating with a wooden spoon until mixture is very smooth.

·3. Combine eggs and egg yolks, and beat gradually into potato mixture. Season to taste with salt, freshly ground black pepper and freshly grated nutmeg, and beat until mixture is very fluffy.

If potatoes are to be used to garnish a meat, fish or vegetable dish, pipe mixture through a pastry tube to make a border, brush with butter and brown under the grill. Or pipe individual shapes with a pastry tube, brush with butter and brown under the grill.

Pommes de Terre en Daube

1 kg/2 lb small new potatoes
100 g/4 oz green bacon, in 1 piece
1 Spanish onion
·4-6 tomatoes
4 tablespoons olive oil
4 level tablespoons tomato purée
1 piece dried orange peel
1 bouquet garni (2 sprigs parsley, 2 sprigs
   thyme, 1 bay leaf)
300 ml/½ pint water or light chicken stock
salt and freshly ground black pepper
finely chopped parsley

1. Peel small new potatoes. If larger ones are used, peel and slice them thickly. Slice bacon thickly

(about 5 mm/¼ inch) and then cut slices into 5-mm/ ¼-inch thick 'fingers'. Chop Spanish onion. Seed and chop tomatoes.

2. Sauté bacon pieces in olive oil until golden; remove bacon and reserve for later use. Sauté chopped onion in remaining fat until transparent. Stir in chopped and seeded tomatoes and tomato purée and cook for a few minutes more. Then add peeled potatoes, bacon bits, orange peel and *bouquet garni* to pan. Add water or chicken stock and salt and freshly ground black pepper, to taste, and simmer until potatoes are tender.

3. Serve garnished with finely chopped parsley.

Oven-baked Potatoes with Soured Cream and Chive Dressing

Illustrated on page 68

4 large baking potatoes
softened butter or olive oil
coarse salt

SOURED CREAM AND CHIVE DRESSING
300 ml/½ pint soured cream
coarsely chopped chives
salt and freshly ground black pepper

1. Scrub the potatoes thoroughly and dry them. Rub with softened butter or olive oil. Sprinkle with coarse salt. Place on a baking tray and bake in a moderately hot oven (190°C, 375°F, Gas Mark 5) for 1½ hours.

2. To make Soured Cream and Chive Dressing: combine 300 ml/½ pint commercial soured cream with 2 to 4 level tablespoons coarsely chopped chives, and season to taste with salt and freshly ground black pepper.

3. Make two deep incisions crossing on top of each cooked potato and then squeeze the base of the potato gently to force the cooked potato inside to emerge.

4. Top with Soured Cream and Chive Dressing, add a sprinkling of chopped chives and serve hot.

Rosti (Swiss Potato Cake)

1 kg/2 lb large potatoes
salt and freshly ground black pepper
4 tablespoons butter
2 tablespoons olive oil

1. Scrub potatoes clean under running water. Place in a large saucepan, cover with water and add salt. Bring to the boil then simmer for 15 minutes, or until potatoes are three-quarters cooked.

2. Drain then cool under running water. Peel off the skins and coarsely grate potatoes into a large bowl. Season well with salt and freshly ground black pepper.

3. Heat butter and olive oil in a large thick-bottomed frying pan. Place grated potatoes in the pan and press lightly into a smooth cake. Season generously with salt and freshly ground black pepper. Cover pan and cook over a medium heat for 8 to 10 minutes.

4. Remove cover and continue cooking for 5 minutes or until bottom of potato cake is crusty and brown, shaking pan from time to time so potatoes do not stick to the pan. Add a little more olive oil or butter if necessary.

5. To serve: turn potato cake out on to a heated serving dish with crusty side up, and cut into thin wedges. Serve immediately.

Pommes Sarladaise

450 g/1 lb new potatoes
4 level tablespoons goose fat, lard or
**   softened butter**
salt and freshly ground black pepper
black truffles, thinly sliced

1. Rub a frying pan generously with goose fat, lard or softened butter.

2. Peel and slice potatoes thinly and soak in cold water for a few minutes. Drain and dry thoroughly with a clean tea towel.

3. Place a layer of sliced potatoes on bottom of frying pan in overlapping rows. Sprinkle with salt and freshly ground black pepper, to taste, and add a few thin slices of black truffle. Repeat until pan is filled, or potatoes are used up, finishing with a layer of potatoes.

3. Cover potatoes with a plate to weight them and to keep moisture in, and sauté them over a gentle heat until bottom layer is crisp and golden, adding a little more fat or butter from time to time, if necessary.

4. Turn potatoes like a pancake and cook again (without the plate) until potatoes are cooked through and nicely browned on both sides. Turn out potato cake and serve immediately.

Buttered Spinach with Ham

1 kg/2 lb fresh spinach leaves
butter
salt and freshly ground black pepper
4-6 level tablespoons diced cooked ham
4-6 level tablespoons diced white bread

1. Wash spinach leaves in several changes of water. Drain.

2. Put spinach in a thick-bottomed saucepan with 225 g/8 oz butter, season to taste with salt and freshly ground black pepper, and cook, stirring constantly, over a fairly high heat until spinach is soft and melted. Transfer to a serving dish and keep warm.

3. Melt 2 tablespoons butter in a frying pan and toss diced ham and diced bread in butter until golden.

4. Fold ham and *croûtons* into spinach, and serve at once as a separate vegetable course.

81

82

Italian Baked Tomatoes and Leeks

4-8 tomatoes, according to size, peeled
4 leeks
4 level tablespoons butter
6 tablespoons dry white wine
$\frac{1}{2}$ chicken stock cube
4 level tablespoons finely chopped fresh
  basil or chives
salt and freshly ground black pepper
olive oil
1 egg yolk
150 ml/$\frac{1}{4}$ pint double cream
4 level tablespoons freshly grated Parmesan
  cheese

1. Preheat oven to moderate (190°C, 375°F, Gas Mark 5).

2. Cut tomatoes in half and gently press out seeds and water. Trim and wash leeks and cut into 2.5-cm/1-inch pieces.

3. Place leeks with butter and dry white wine and $\frac{1}{2}$ chicken stock cube, crumbled, in a large shallow flameproof *gratin* dish. Sprinkle leeks with finely chopped fresh basil or chives and season with salt and freshly ground black pepper. Bake in a preheated oven for 10 minutes.

4. Season peeled tomatoes with salt and freshly ground black pepper and arrange them, cut-side

Grilled Italian Tomatoes

6 large ripe tomatoes
butter
salt and freshly ground black pepper
dried oregano
2 level tablespoons breadcrumbs
2 level teaspoons finely chopped chives
  or onion
2 level tablespoons freshly grated Parmesan
  cheese

1. Cut tomatoes in half.

2. Place tomato halves in a buttered baking dish. Season to taste with salt, freshly ground black pepper and dried oregano. Sprinkle with breadcrumbs, finely chopped chives or onion and freshly grated Parmesan. Dot tomatoes with butter and grill them 7.5 cm/3 inches from the heat until tender.

down, on top of the leeks. Brush with olive oil; return dish to oven and cook for 10 more minutes.

5. Beat egg yolk and double cream together and spoon over vegetables. Sprinkle with freshly grated Parmesan and continue to cook until sauce is bubbling and lightly browned.

Green Souffléd Tomatoes

8 medium-sized tomatoes, or 4 very large
   tomatoes
salt and freshly ground black pepper
100 g/4 oz frozen spinach, defrosted
butter
1 (85-g/3-oz) packet Philadelphia cream
   cheese, diced
6 level tablespoons double cream
2 egg yolks, beaten
4–5 level tablespoons freshly grated
   Parmesan cheese
cayenne
olive oil
4 egg whites
dry white wine

1. Preheat oven to moderately hot (200°C, 400°F, Gas Mark 6).

2. Slice tops off tomatoes, scoop out interiors carefully and discard. Season insides of tomatoes generously with salt and freshly ground black pepper. Drain tomato cases upside down in refrigerator for at least 30 minutes.

3. Heat spinach with a little butter and purée in an electric blender. Drain.

4. Beat cream cheese with double cream until smooth. Add beaten egg yolks and puréed spinach and season with freshly grated Parmesan and salt, freshly ground black pepper and cayenne, to taste.

5. Brush tomato cases, inside and out, with olive oil and heat through in oven.

6. Beat egg whites until stiff. Gently fold into spinach and cheese mixture.

7. Pile mixture into tomato cases and place in a flameproof *gratin* dish. Add a little olive oil and dry white wine to moisten bottom of dish. Bring liquid to the boil on top of the cooker, then cook tomato soufflés in preheated oven for 5 minutes. Reduce heat to moderate (160°C, 325°F, Gas Mark 3) and continue to cook for 10 to 15 minutes, until well risen and cooked through.

Tomatoes Stuffed with Mussels

8–12 firm tomatoes
salt and freshly ground black pepper
1 Spanish onion, finely chopped
1 clove garlic, finely chopped
4 level tablespoons finely chopped parsley
6 button mushrooms, finely chopped
4–6 anchovy fillets, finely chopped
olive oil
6 level tablespoons fresh breadcrumbs
8–12 mussels
dry white wine
butter

1. Cut a slice from the stem end of each tomato and scoop out the seeds with a spoon. Season insides of tomatoes generously with salt and freshly ground black pepper and turn them upside down to drain.

2. Sauté finely chopped onion, garlic, parsley, mushrooms and anchovies in 4 tablespoons olive oil until vegetables are brown. Stir in half the fresh breadcrumbs, season with salt and freshly ground black pepper and simmer mixture for 5 more minutes.

3. Scrub mussels, remove beards and stem in a little dry white wine until mussels open. Remove mussels from shells, discarding any that have not opened. Strain mussel liquor into sauce. Chop mussels finely and stir into sauce.

4. Arrange the prepared tomatoes in a buttered baking dish and stuff them with the mussel and breadcrumb mixture. Sprinkle with remaining breadcrumbs and a few drops of olive oil. Brown the topping in a moderately hot oven (200°C, 400°F, Gas Mark 6).

84

Buttered Turnip and Carrot Strips

675 g/1½ lb turnips
675 g/1½ lb carrots
salt and freshly ground black pepper
4 level tablespoons butter
8 tablespoons chicken stock
2 level tablespoons finely chopped parsley

1. Wash and trim turnips and carrots and cut into thin strips about 5 mm/¼ inch in diameter and of equal length. Season generously with salt and freshly ground black pepper.

2. Simmer gently in butter and a little stock until just tender.

3. Sprinkle with finely chopped parsley and serve immediately.

Creamed Turnip, Carrot and Cucumber Strips

450 g/1 lb turnips
450 g/1 lb carrots
salt and freshly ground black pepper
1 cucumber
4 level tablespoons butter
2 tablespoons olive oil
6-8 level tablespoons double cream
2 level tablespoons chopped chives

1. Prepare turnips and carrots as in Step **1.** of Buttered Turnip and Carrot Strips (see recipe above).

2. Peel cucumber, cut in half and scoop out seeds. Cut it into thin strips the same size as turnip and carrot strips.

3. Simmer vegetables gently in butter and olive oil until just tender. Add double cream and heat through. Sprinkle with chopped chives and serve immediately.

Gratin of Young Turnips

675 g/1½ lb small French turnips
2 level tablespoons butter
1 egg
150 ml/¼ pint double cream
8 level tablespoons freshly grated Gruyère cheese
4 level tablespoons freshly grated Parmesan cheese
salt and freshly ground black pepper

1. Peel or scrape turnips and slice them very thinly (about 1.5 mm/$\frac{1}{16}$ inch thick). Rinse thoroughly and leave to soak in a bowl of cold water for 15 minutes. Select a shallow ovenproof dish about 23 cm/9 inches by 13 cm/5 inches. Grease with 2 level teaspoons of the butter.

2. Drain turnip slices and dry them thoroughly with a cloth or absorbent paper. Whisk egg and cream until well blended.

3. Arrange a quarter of the turnip slices in the dish in overlapping rows. Pour over 2 level tablespoons egg and cream mixture and sprinkle with 2 level tablespoons Gruyère and 1 level tablespoon Parmesan. Dot with 1 level teaspoon butter and, finally, season to taste with salt and freshly ground black pepper.

4. Repeat layers exactly as above, making four in all, and ending with grated cheese and butter.

5. Bake *gratin* in a cool oven (150°C, 300°F, Gas Mark 2) for 1 hour 20 minutes, or until turnips feel tender when pierced with a sharp skewer and are golden and bubbling on top.

6. Allow to 'settle' for a few minutes before serving.

Note: If top browns too quickly, cover with a sheet of foil.

Stuffed Green Peppers (see page 77)

Chinese Braised Vegetables (see page 63)

Chinese Spinach (see page 63)

Broccoli with Cheese Sauce and Slivered Almonds (see page 55)

Mushrooms en Brochette (see page 73)

Sauces

Hollandaise Sauce

1 teaspoon lemon juice
1 tablespoon cold water
salt and white pepper
100 g/4 oz soft butter
4 egg yolks
lemon juice

1. Combine lemon juice, water, salt and white pepper in the top of a double saucepan or *bain-marie*.

2. Divide butter into four equal pieces.

3. Add the egg yolks and a quarter of the butter to the liquid in the saucepan, and stir the mixture rapidly and constantly with a wire whisk over hot, but not boiling, water until the butter is melted and the mixture begins to thicken. Add the second piece of butter and continue whisking. As the mixture thickens and the second piece of butter melts, add the third piece of butter, stirring from the bottom of the pan until it is melted. Be careful not to allow the water over which the sauce is cooking to boil at any time. Add rest of butter, beating until it melts and is incorporated in the sauce.

4. Remove top part of saucepan from heat and continue to beat for 2 to 3 minutes. Replace saucepan over hot, but not boiling, water for 2 minutes more, beating constantly. By this time the emulsion should have formed and your sauce will be rich and creamy. 'Finish' sauce with a few drops of lemon juice. Strain and serve.

Note: If at any time in the operation the mixture should curdle, beat in 1 or 2 tablespoons cold water to rebind the emulsion.

Béchamel Sauce

butter
$\frac{1}{2}$ onion, minced
2 tablespoons flour
600 ml/1 pint hot milk
2 tablespoons lean veal or ham, chopped
1 small sprig thyme
$\frac{1}{2}$ bay leaf
white peppercorns
freshly grated nutmeg

1. In a thick-bottomed saucepan, or in the top of a double saucepan, melt 2 tablespoons butter and cook onion in it over a low heat until transparent. Stir in flour and cook for a few minutes, stirring constantly, until mixture cooks through but does not take on colour.

2. Gradually add hot milk and cook, stirring constantly, until the mixture is thick and smooth.

3. In another saucepan, simmer finely chopped lean veal or ham in 1 tablespoon butter over a very low heat. Season with thyme, bay leaf, white peppercorns and grated nutmeg. Cook for 5 minutes, stirring to keep veal from browning.

4. Add veal to the sauce and cook over hot water for 45 minutes to 1 hour, stirring occasionally. When reduced to the proper consistency (two-thirds of the original quantity), strain sauce through a fine sieve into a bowl, pressing meat and onion well to extract all the liquid. Cover surface of sauce with tiny pieces of butter to keep film from forming.

Note: For a richer Béchamel, remove the saucepan from the heat, add 1 or 2 egg yolks, and heat through. Do not let sauce come to the boil after adding eggs or it will curdle.

89

90

Raw Tomato Sauce

(Excellent for pasta and fish dishes.)

1.25 kg/2½ lb ripe tomatoes
1 large Spanish onion
1 clove garlic
3 tablespoons olive oil
3 level tablespoons finely chopped fresh basil
3 level tablespoons finely chopped fresh chives
salt and freshly ground black pepper

1. Quarter tomatoes. Peel and quarter onion. Peel garlic and cut in half.

2. Place onion and garlic pieces in an electric blender with olive oil and blend until finely chopped. Add quartered tomatoes and finely chopped herbs and blend until sauce is smooth. Season with salt and freshly ground black pepper, to taste. Chill until ready to use.

French Tomato Sauce

2 level tablespoons butter
4 level tablespoons finely chopped ham
1 small carrot, finely chopped
1 small turnip, finely chopped
1 onion, finely chopped
1 stick celery, finely chopped
6-8 ripe tomatoes, sliced
2 level tablespoons tomato purée
1 level tablespoon flour
1 bouquet garni (1 sprig each thyme, marjoram and parsley)
300 ml/½ pint well-flavoured beef stock
salt and freshly ground black pepper
lemon juice
sugar

1. Melt butter in a thick-bottomed saucepan; add finely chopped ham and vegetables, and sauté mixture until onion is transparent and soft.

2. Stir in sliced tomatoes and tomato purée and simmer for a minute or two. Sprinkle with flour and mix well. Then add *bouquet garni* and beef stock, and simmer gently, stirring continuously,

until sauce comes to the boil. Skim sauce; season to taste with salt and freshly ground black pepper, and simmer gently for 30 minutes, stirring from time to time. If the sauce becomes too thick, add a little more stock.

3. Strain sauce through a fine sieve. Reheat and add lemon juice and sugar, to taste.

English Onion Sauce

2 Spanish onions, quartered
4 level tablespoons butter
2 tablespoons flour
½ chicken stock cube, crumbled
150 ml/¼ pint milk or single cream
salt and freshly ground black pepper
pinch of nutmeg

1. Boil onions until tender and drain well, reserving onion liquor. Chop onions finely. Reserve.

2. Melt butter in the top of a double saucepan. Remove pan from heat, stir in flour and ½ chicken stock cube; crumbled; return to heat and cook gently for 3 to 5 minutes, stirring constantly, until the flour is cooked through. Add milk (or single cream), heated to boiling point, and cook over water, stirring constantly, until sauce starts to thicken.

3. Add chopped onions, 150 ml/¼ pint reserved onion liquor, and salt, freshly ground black pepper and nutmeg, to taste. Heat through.

Mushroom Sauce Suprême

5 level tablespoons butter
2 level tablespoons flour
600 ml/1 pint boiling chicken stock
100 g/4 oz button mushrooms, finely chopped
100 g/4 oz button mushrooms, thinly sliced
150 ml/¼ pint double cream
Madeira
salt and cayenne

1. Melt 4 level tablespoons butter in the top of a double saucepan and blend in the flour thoroughly, being very careful not to let it colour.

2. Remove saucepan from heat and pour in the boiling stock. Cook over water, stirring constantly, until it thickens slightly. Add finely chopped mushrooms and simmer for 10 to 15 minutes, stirring from time to time.

3. Strain sauce, forcing mushrooms and onion through a fine sieve. Add sliced mushrooms, double cream and Madeira, to taste, and cook over a low heat until mushrooms are tender. Season to taste with salt and a little cayenne.

4. Remove sauce from the heat and whisk in the remaining butter, adding it in small pieces.

If the sauce is not to be used immediately, put several dabs of butter on top to prevent a skin forming.

Mayonnaise

91

2 egg yolks
salt and freshly ground black pepper
½ level teaspoon Dijon mustard
lemon juice
300 ml/½ pint olive oil

1. Place egg yolks (make sure gelatinous thread of the egg is removed), salt, freshly ground black pepper and mustard in a bowl. Twist a cloth wrung out in very cold water round the bottom of the bowl to keep it steady and cool. Using a wire whisk, fork or wooden spoon, beat the yolks to a smooth paste.

2. Add a little lemon juice (the acid helps the emulsion), and beat in about a quarter of the oil, drop by drop. Add a little more lemon juice to the mixture and then, a little more quickly now, add more oil, beating all the while. Continue adding oil and beating until the sauce is of a good thick consistency. Correct seasoning (more salt, freshly ground black pepper and lemon juice) as desired. If you are making the mayonnaise a day before using it, stir in 1 tablespoon boiling water when it is of the desired consistency. This will keep it from turning or separating.

Note: If the mayonnaise should curdle, break another egg yolk into a clean bowl and gradually beat the curdled mayonnaise into it. Your mayonnaise will begin to 'take' immediately.

If mayonnaise is to be used for a salad, thin it down considerably with dry white wine, vinegar or lemon juice. If it is to be used for coating meat, poultry or fish, add a little liquid aspic to stiffen it.

If mayonnaise is to be kept for several hours before serving, cover the bowl with a cloth wrung out in very cold water to prevent a skin from forming on the top.

Index